tea from a jam jar

tea from a jam jar

Heart warming and sometimes sad, this is a story of rejection heaped on despair

By Alfie Watson

tea from a jam jar *Alfie Watson*

Copyright © 2014 Alfie Watson
All rights reserved.
ISBN 10: 1502885239
ISBN 13: 978 1502885234

DEDICATION

I want to say a special thank you to my wife Karen who has shown me the path to happiness and contentment. And who is wholly responsible for steering me away from an almost inevitable life of crime.

tea from a jam jar   *Alfie Watson*

Contents

1. The early Years
2. New Queen
3. Winter
4. My duties
5. A visitor
6. My second school
7. The giggles
8. Death
9. The telly
10. Trolley races
11. My first holiday
12. Detector vans
13. Sex instructions
14. The bullet
15. Gardening
16. The army cadets
17. Sad day
18. Next step is work
19. Humiliation
20. A lesson about life
21. Special Birthday
22. My lovely gran
23. Ice creams
24. Motorbikes and cars
25. Brag
26. I meet Karen
27. Bully of a father
28. On the roof
29. Blackpool
30. The proposal
31. The wedding

tea from a jam jar *Alfie Watson*

FOREWORD

This book has been written in a chronological form in an attempt to convey to the reader certain situations that have arisen during the young impressionable years of the author's life. The compilation therefore may lack depth of flow in the extremely early years of his life and may appear rather more descriptive than narrative.

Please stick with it!

INTRODUCTION

My story begins at the district Hospital in Lisburn, County Antrim on March 25th 1945, and the year of my birth. I was duly Christened Alfie after my father. He was a serving soldier in the Royal Artillery stationed at the Thiepval Barracks Northern Ireland, where he met and married my mother, Sue Kidd, an Irish woman from the majority protestant side of Lisburn, a town situated just south east of Belfast. I have no recollection of my early days in Northern Ireland; I understand that my parents lived in married quarters until demobilisation at the end of the war. The next few years of marriage were spent in lodgings, with members of my

tea from a jam jar   *Alfie Watson*

mothers family. In 1950, along with my sisters Sue and Christine I was brought to England. This is my story about growing up on a council estate in Leicester, England from my arrival, age 5 up to my 20th Birthday in 1965.

tea from a jam jar *Alfie Watson*

tea from a jam jar   *Alfie Watson*

One

THE EARLY YEARS

My first memories of Leicester were of our time spent lodging with my dad's sister, Pearl. I remember her with great affection, she was a lovely lady and extremely pretty with long blonde hair. Her husband, Ted had also recently been demobilised from the army and they had also married shortly afterwards. It must have put quite a strain on them though, to be lumbered with us so soon into their married life. This house was incredibly small, cold and cramped. These properties were referred to as "back to back terraces". It had two bedrooms and one downstairs room where the food was prepared over the only fire grate in the house. To call it basic was a definite under statement. Four adults and three kids sharing two tiny bedrooms was not conducive to a happy start to married life for either my uncle and aunt or my parents. Then there was the added problem of sharing toilet facilities with several neighbouring properties. I think there were three toilets shared between six houses that were, lets say, not quite as concerned about hygiene as we were. This led to many arguments between the various families. There was, I remember a small yard which again was shared by all of the properties. It was no more than about three or four metres square and very cluttered. I think because each family considered that the space immediately outside their back door

tea from a jam jar   *Alfie Watson*

was their backyard, anything that became surplus to their requirements found itself lying there. So basically the area resembled a tip. I don't think we stayed there too long before we moved in with my dad's parents on the Braunstone Estate where we shared a house with my uncles Gerry and Alan and my auntie Joan. The things that stay in my memory the most about our stay there are of my grandma's bread pudding, a goose and a bull mastiff dog named Rover and soaking wet towels. The latter being that there was an abundance of kids and a distinct shortage of towels with which to dry them. Any towels available were always soaking wet and dirty anyway because they were in constant use as tea towels.

The goose was allowed a free run of the back garden and woe betide anyone who tried to enter, even rover kept his distance from this vicious creature.

Although the house was a post war semi detached property, it had an entry or passage way which led to the back gardens. Whenever anyone walked down the entry, the goose would react wildly to the sound of the echoing footsteps as the dog barked loudly from the safety of the house. You'd have to have been mental to enter while this pair was on the loose.

Bread pudding was a favourite of most homes in those days. It was supposed to be a pudding but it was so filling it was mostly used as the main meal. From what I remember, it was basically stale left over bread with currants mixed in and milk poured over it and finally baked. I thought it was lovely, but then nobody cooked it like my gran.

tea from a jam jar   *Alfie Watson*

This house was so much bigger than auntie Pearl's with three bedrooms and a garden to play in, only when the goose was locked up of course. Even so, the headcount was still ten during the week and eleven at weekends, when my granddad made his only appearance of the week.

He was an old soldier who'd seen action in the first world war when serving in the Somme. Although he had considered himself lucky to have come through it relatively unscathed, he did suffer from shrapnel wounds to his ankle, which he was clearly still having problems with some thirty years on. He worked for a tarmacadam company laying road surfaces around the country. The fact that he was working away during the week, helped to ease the current population problem somewhat, but these crowded conditions couldn't have been easy for my mam or my grandma. Even so, throughout our stay, I cannot remember hearing a cross word or a voice raised in anger from either my mam or my grandma.

My mam was, I suppose, a medium built woman with a ruddy farmer's wife sort of complexion. She had an extremely hard faced appearance, this combined with a strong Irish temperament made her an extremely unaffectionate and sometimes a very volatile person. I was never ever talked too, but always shouted at, by her; in fact I'm quite sure that I never saw her smile, ever. She possessed a very dominant controlling personality, which my dad regularly bore the brunt of. My grandma on the other hand, well she was a smashing lady, standing all of five feet tall with a mop of white hair and a ready smile. With her brightly flowered aprons, she epitomised everyone's idea of the perfect gran.

We stayed with grandma for about a month before moving to a house of our own. This new house was just around the corner. By this time I had acquired a brother, Horace.

Now 43 Bendbow Rise was to be my home for the next fourteen years or so. This move was no doubt given priority by the housing department after another uncle, who I haven't mentioned yet, returned home on leave. Brian was his name and he was the next eldest son after my dad. He was serving in the army with the Leicestershire Tigers in Malaya at the time, and arrived unexpectedly to find his bed occupied. He hadn't been due home on leave for some months so his arrival played havoc with the sleeping arrangements, but as usual, we managed somehow.

As with most kids, I had a favourite uncle, his name was Gerry, aged about seventeen, he was tall, but then compared to me, who wasn't? Well built with a chiselled jaw line and piercing blue eyes, he always dipped his hand in his pocket whenever he saw me, always producing sweets or a few pennies. Brian was just as generous to us, whenever he was home on leave, as were my other uncles and aunts, I can't explain this affinity with Gerry, but I always felt closer to him. I was soon going to miss him, as it was time for him to follow in his brothers footsteps and do his two years of national service.

Our new house was not too crowded, two to each bedroom was just nice, but that wasn't to last for very long. The

tea from a jam jar — Alfie Watson

neighbours of my grandma's had just seen one of their sons married, and he and his new wife were now looking for a room to rent. This seemed to be the order in which things happened in those times, get wed and then start to look for a place to live. They moved in with us taking over the second biggest room in the house, which I suppose was to be expected but it left us four kids to share the smallest one. The house suddenly became a very crowded and inhospitable place, with my mam and the lodgers constantly arguing and bickering. We woke to arguing and went to bed with it too.

My sister Sue was now almost ten years old and along with Christine really needed to be in a room on her own, as did Horace and myself. Whether or not our guests also felt this, I don't know but it wasn't too long before they, thankfully found somewhere else to live allowing us to get back to some sort of normality.

It was now time for me to start attending school or rather nursery. I know that every child is unhappy about attending for the first day and I was no different. Although I don't remember joining in with the bawling and screaming that went on at the school gates, as some kids refused to let go of their mothers hands. But I did know instinctively that I was not going to like it very much, and would go to great lengths to avoid going back again each day.

The one thing I hated most of all was being put to bed in the afternoon. As far as I was concerned, sleeping was something that should be done at night, although I was never that keen to do it then either. I can remember shedding many tears and having really violent tantrums over this matter. This prompted the teacher, Mrs. Cramp, a small middle aged, upright bespectacled lady who wore her hair in a strange style that, I thought resembled a pair of large headphones, to regularly send for my mother, who would then invariably take me back home. It wasn't long before my mam got fed up with this and I was punished accordingly, with a damned good smack on the backside and head. It seems on reflection that I would do anything to bring grief on that teacher, and I don't really know why because she was very nice really. Another ploy of mine at that time was to deliberately get my hands dirty whilst walking to school but not before making sure that my mam had checked them before I left home. Hand inspection was the first duty of the day for Mrs. Cramp, and she was very meticulous, and not surprisingly directed me straight to the wash room. It's a wonder she didn't suspect what I was up to, because apart from my hands, which were caked in mud, I was otherwise immaculate - by my standards that is - and would stay that way, at least for the first ten minutes or so. My story to my mam would be that I was constantly being picked on for not being clean. She would not take this kind of criticism lying down, and would tell the teacher so in no uncertain terms, while I stood angelically by her side.

I don't have that many bad memories of nursery school, other than those mentioned, generally they were happy days, when the sun seemed to always shine and days seemed to go on forever. The most important thing that mattered then was that my little apron, with its acorn motif was hanging on its peg when I arrived. The next and possibly equally important, after the calling of the register, was to make sure I got to the sandpit first.

On Sunday's, we had to attend Sunday school. All of us kids had to wear our best clothes on that very special day, and I must say we looked pretty good, at least on the outside. It's a good job no one could see my underpants though, they would more often than not, either be full of holes or, on some occasions, they would belong to one of my sisters. We would all stride proudly up to the school, my sisters and me, listen to the scriptures, sing some songs receive our text and head back home again. The text was a small glossy picture portraying some religious event or person, and was to be stuck into our own personal textbook on the appropriate page, just as youngsters today save pictures of footballers or film stars. We were always excited to receive them. Returning home at around 3 o'clock, it wasn't unusual to find mam and dad in bed. So really, sending us off to Sunday school was their clever way of getting time together.

Two

DEATH

It's now 1952 and as a lively seven year old I was about to get my first introduction to death. My granddad, a very heavy smoker died of lung cancer in August of this year. He had been ill for some time and had been in and out of hospital during the previous years, the last time to have a lung removed. It was said at the time, that his life had already been somewhat extended by virtue of the newly discovered medical benefit of the asphalt fumes he had been inhaling during his later years working on the roads.

My lasting memory was of him lying in bed while I placed pieces of orange into his toothless mouth, feeding him a segment at a time. I wasn't to know then that this would be the last time I'd see him. I knew he was poorly but in my childhood world I thought that everybody recovered from illness. This awful time had a noticeable effect on everyone, not least my lovely grandma. She would never really be quite the same again.

Another death in that same year was that of King George VI, the father of our present Queen. This must have come as a shock to the adults at this time. Of course I didn't understand what it was all about at my age. I can remember, as I made my way to school after lunch, clearly hearing radios, their volumes turned up, echoing through open doors

tea from a jam jar   *Alfie Watson*

as the lunchtime news announced his death. People were visibly upset and women could be seen openly crying in the street.

   I think I should describe the geography surrounding 43 Bendbow Rise. As the address suggests, our house was situated on a hill, a little over half way up in fact. My school was only about 150 yards from my home, near to the top end of the hill. The daily walk to school took about 5 minutes, and involved crossing Hand Avenue, a very busy road which was also a bus route but nevertheless, along with my sisters, we were expected to get there on our own. This fact alone shows how independent we all would have to become. To follow the footpaths to school would have taken a chicane type route, which in later years was used as a racetrack for our home made racing trolleys. The direct way took us over the main road onto a grassed area that would lead almost to the school gates, with just a small problem of crossing another road at the top part of Bendbow Rise. To travel in the southerly direction for 100 yards would find you standing in front of a giant oak tree, an object that would feature regularly in my nightmares. These would almost always involved me falling and falling endlessly into some sort of abyss, with my head swollen to about twice its normal size. I would always wake up, terrified, before I had reached the bottom. For which I'm pretty sure one of the modern day dream readers would have had a perfectly logical explanation. From this tree the road split left and right either side of a grassed play area and continued for about three hundred yards where it met another main road, which was even busier than Hand Avenue. This road separated the whole estate from the Braunstone Park. Here is where the American servicemen had been stationed during the war years. They had long since returned home, leaving behind a skeleton staff to oversee the transformation from barracks back to parkland, a task that was to take several more years, judging by the mess to this area of the park.

tea from a jam jar *Alfie Watson*

Three

NEW QUEEN

A party to celebrate the coronation of Queen Elizabeth was being arranged on the estate and these were very exciting times to be at school, there seemed to be an air of happiness everywhere. Bunting trimmed the streets and the talk was all about parties, of which every street had one. As this generally meant that whole streets were closed to traffic, it must have presented the council with a logistical nightmare. It was decided that Hand Avenue would be the venue for all the children in our area, even though it was a very busy bus route. This road, with its grassed area on either side- but no trees as its name might suggest - was the perfect setting for a street party. Rows of tables, each catering for about thirty excited kids, were spaced along both sides of the avenue to within about two hundred yards of the police box (the tardis, which you'll read more about later) and stopping just past my grandma's house in the opposite direction. At the party I recall having a really great time, with so much food that many of us would end up feeling very ill indeed and some were physically sick. After all, this type of food along with fresh cream and ice cream, was totally alien to most of us so we obviously took the opportunity to fill our boots There was more food than I had ever seen in my life, and lots, as I say, that I could not even recognise. There were scores of us kids, all seated at long benches with coronation hats and flags, with the adult relatives of the various kids, doing the serving.

We were there on one side of the avenue, so my grandparents along with auntie Joan and uncle Alan had made sure that they were on the other. Showing me and the rest of the neighbours that there was a rift of some sort going on that they would probably never have otherwise noticed.

As I said it was a really exciting time to be a kid, with every child receiving a coronation mug from the school to take home. Other souvenirs such as spoons, toothbrushes and coins etc. could be collected from the various parties and school treats that were in abundance all around the estate.

Four

WINTER

Home, was always extremely cold in the winter months, when only one room ever felt warm and that was the living room or lounge. The bedroom I shared with my brother had a fire grate, but this was only lit when another birth was imminent. We were then all shuffled around like cards into different rooms. When the baby arrived and the midwife had done whatever it was a midwife did, normality would be resumed.

The coldness of that house might explain why I was caught on a couple of occasions with a box of matches, trying to start a fire in the corner of the living room. For some reason I would collect a small pile of screwed up newspaper, which I'd stack against the skirting board and proceed to set fire to it. My mam's response to this naturally, was to hit out at me with whatever she could put her hands on at the time. This was quite often done with a rolled up newspaper or magazine, and the blows were always aimed at my head and ears with some venom and always accompanied by the warning, "just you wait till your dad gets home," I'd then have to spend the rest of the day in fear of his arrival. I was given a constant update during the day as to how long it would be before he was due home. By which time, I'd be totally petrified, and would hide away behind a chair or under the table often wetting myself with fear. I knew it wouldn't be too difficult for him to find me but I think this was just a token gesture on my part, hoping that if he saw that I was in such awe of him, then maybe, just maybe, he might consider this to be punishment enough. But his reaction was always the same; he'd chastise me severely with the help of a thick leather belt to my bare backside and a couple of whacks around the ears with the flat of his hand for good measure. Unfortunately this didn't stop me, and I was soon caught in action again. This time it was decided to involve the police.

Sitting in the heart of the estate, not too far from my grandma's house, was a blue coloured police box, looking not unlike the 'tardis' used in the 'Dr Who' series. From here the local bobby would communicate with the main police station in the town centre. This is where I was dragged by my dad, to be confronted by a very large policeman and I remember quite clearly sitting petrified in a chair inside the 'tardis' with this huge man towering over me. He warned me over and over again that unless I saw the error of my ways, I could be sent away somewhere where I would be punished. Finishing his lecture with the repeated line, do you understand boy, and me nodding frantically. The threat of going to prison was a frightening thought to a now eight year old child. It worked and my days as an arsonist were well and truly over, I never lit fires in the house again. Neither did I ever understand why I did it in the first place.

Bedtimes were nearly always preceded by an argument over who was to have dads old army greatcoat, which would be found hanging over the banister, and doubled as an extra blanket. I have quite clear memories of our bedroom and the bed I shared with Horace. Sleeping in a standard size bed was pretty much the norm now but unfortunately did not always lead to a good night sleep.

Horace, now aged about three years old would often go for a walk in the night – something he would do until he reached his teens – and would almost always wet the bed. On waking in the mornings the back of my pyjamas would very often be soaking wet. This along with the coldness of the room, especially during the winter months, was not the ideal way to start the day. I remember it being so cold in our room that the windows would be just as frosty on the inside as they were on the outside. We used to get dressed as soon as we got out of bed, in order to get warm. Any wash would take place downstairs but that would only be hands and face. Boy, I must have been a smelly little bastard. Come to think of it, I can recall being called wee wee Watson a few times but never made the connection.

Beds were being moved around again and this could only mean one thing, a new sibling was on the way. Another boy, Peter, had arrived.

Five

MY DUTIES

Bath times were another interesting time back then and the process could last for several hours and usually took place on Sunday evening after Sunday school. The bathwater had to be heated in a large cast iron drum that we knew as the copper which was situated in the corner of the kitchen. When the water in the copper was ready, and this would take a lot of boiling and many coins in the gas meter, it then had to be transferred via a pump, situated in the kitchen, into the bath. This device, while being very temperamental, also required a good deal of strength by the person doing the pumping. As the eldest boy this task fell to me and would become one of my biggest hates and clearest memories. This hopeless contraption needed to be primed by pouring a small amount of cold water into an eggcup shaped vessel attached to the pump. The water would not pump through to the bath until a certain pressure was reached. This, I remember, seemed to take forever and a day and extraordinary amount of patience, not only by me but also by the one waiting, shivering in the cold bathroom, for their bathwater to arrive. But at least they knew that the water would be clean when they did get it, so well worth the wait. Only one copper full of water was allowed for all of us. As there was three other siblings, I would be fourth in line. The bath, by this time was not very inviting at all, in fact it looked and smelt more like a stagnant pond and was barely warm. I swear every last one of them had pissed in it. But nevertheless, I was made to get in it and go through the motions. But it would be no more than a token gesture. In and out like a drowning tomcat. I suppose it was better than no bath at all.

Looking back on those days I really did draw the short straw. Having already exhausted myself pumping the water through and having to hang around until my turn came along, I then had the job of cleaning out the bath which was caked with a thick black greasy messy substance that would refuse to budge from the sides of the bath without the help of some scouring powder sprinkled onto a wire scouring pad.

The kitchen was where we would wash and sometimes change on weekdays before leaving for school. Dominating this room and facing the door from the passage, was a large pine table covered with an oilcloth. For my younger readers, this was a tablecloth, which had been treated during manufacture in a type of plastic, finish which proved to be extremely functional and common in most homes in those days. The table was laid 24/7. Featuring on our typical table would be a part used bottle of milk, a part loaf of sliced bread, sugar, margarine, mixed fruit or lemon curd jam, brown sauce a couple of used knives covered in margarine or jam, or both. Several flies and the occasional ant, oh! I almost forgot the mouse droppings which were sometimes in the sugar bowl and also around the table. Why we didn't get food poisoning I'll never understand.

This table and its contents were available to us any time of the day. We'd spread our bread directly onto the oilcloth or the palm of our hand as there were no plates available to us. Our hands were probably cleanest option. Usually our sandwiches consisted of margarine and mixed fruit jam, margarine and brown sauce or margarine and sugar with the latter being dipped directly into the sugar bowl. This would explain why, when we would have a drink of tea with sugar in - often from a jam jar because there was a shortage of cups – it would have a greasy substance floating on top. On some occasions I vaguely remember having condensed milk or pork dripping which had come from dad's favourite, "pigs head" which he had for his own delectation now and then. Once the bread had gone, that was it! you would starve until a meal time, assuming of course we had one.

Occasionally we were given a few broken biscuits to fill us, which incidentally always ended in arguments as everyone wanted the cream ones. These biscuits came in a large square silver tin and were the rejects from a manufacturer somewhere in town. They were sold at the local shop but were sold out as soon as they hit the shelves. These were a good substitute for bread and very popular around the streets of the estate. By the way, my favourites were custard creams(and they still are) and cream wafers but sadly they seemed to be everyone else's too!

Hanging directly over the kitchen table was a flytrap. This was a strip of brown paper covered in a sticky substance. The idea being, that the flies and wasps would be attracted to it by the treacle like scent and once they had landed on it they were stuck fast, hence, during the summer, a constant feature of the kitchen was this persistent buzzing noise of insects attempting to set themselves free.

Under the window was the Belfast sink where the morning wash, or should that be rinse? took place; sometimes we'd use the same water that the dishes were soaking in. There was no hot running water, so whatever we needed had to be boiled in a saucepan on the stove, and this took time and money, neither of which we seemed to have very much of. Soap was usually Fairy, Sunlight or Lifebuoy carbolic and could be found sharing a dish on the windowsill with a rusty scouring pad along with my dad's shaving razor. This soap had almost certainly been used to scrub floors and also to wash clothes. My mam would scrub the collars of my dads shirts with it on the wooden draining board, while I waited patiently for her to finish, so I could have a wash. It wasn't unusual to find particles of rusty wire from the scouring pad, embedded in it, so I was wise to check it thoroughly before using it.

Opposite the kitchen table stood the cooker or oven; this acted as a heater in the winter mornings, when it would be lit and the door left open. On top of the cooker, a metal teapot would always be found simmering during waking hours. It was switched off at bedtime and filled and relit in the morning. My mother imported this practice of "stewing" tea, from Ireland. As soon as the last cup was emptied from it, more tea leaves would be added to those already there along with cold water, before being placed back on the stove on a low light. I had a real liking for stewed tea, I suppose partly because there was nothing else, so if you didn't like it you went without. In any case it was so thick it was more like a snack. There was an alternative in the house to the tea, this was "camp coffee" but it was kept high up in the pantry for dad's taste buds only. Directly underneath the cooker on the floor sat an old roasting tray containing quite a large amount of congealed fat that had dripped from the oven during several weeks of cooking the Sunday roast, which incidentally, we only had if dad was working. One glance at the footprints on this would give some indication of how big the mouse population was, too many prints and out would come the traps. These could be heard during the night, snapping closed on some poor unsuspecting rodent's neck. Dad used to set them in the pantry and kitchen floor and table before retiring for the night and with the help of a small amount of cheese or bacon rind, he always got a result.

My parents failed dismally to protect what little food we had from these creatures and seemed unconcerned that our health could be at risk. The only food I can remember being covered over was the cheese which could be found in a really fancy looking cheese dish in the pantry, there along with the coffee, out of the reach of the kids. This again was solely for my dad's consumption. Ironically, it was considered to be vitally important that we were given a daily dose of cod liver oil, malt, and orange juice. These vile remedies were dished out every morning without fail and there was no avoiding it. How I hated that stuff! It was made available on the National

tea from a jam jar   *Alfie Watson*

Health in order to restore all of us back to good health, after the deprivation of the war years. We would form a line and in turn be given a teaspoon full of cod liver oil followed by a tablespoon of malt and to help restore our taste buds back to something resembling normality, a small drink of extremely thick and tasty orange juice. This ritual took place before leaving for school and sometimes doubled as breakfast.

For some reason, known only to my parents, we were now forbidden from visiting any relatives, especially grandma. This obviously meant that uncles and aunts still at home were not seen as often as we kids would have liked. With only about twelve or so houses separating us there were times when we'd unavoidably bump into them in the street, and they would always make a fuss of us, treating us like long lost relatives and really that's precisely what we had become, through no fault of ours. It didn't matter which one of them we'd meet, they always ended up giving us a treat of some sort. They were always careful not to say anything that could antagonise the situation. They also knew that we couldn't be held responsible for our parent's actions. Nevertheless, I was always left with an overwhelming feeling of guilt and worry of what would happen if mam should find out. Because of this, contact was usually quite fleeting.

Six

A VISITOR

It's 1954 and my ninth birthday brings the usual greetings cards and cheap present from mam and dad. When looking back on those days I realise now that money was extremely scarce and therefore it was not unusual to be told that the new shoes or coat that had been given a month or two earlier, courtesy of the welfare state, was in fact my main birthday pressie!

Uncle Brian arrived at our door a few days after my Birthday - looking resplendent in his dress uniform - bearing a neatly wrapped parcel. He had been back to serve his Queen and country in Malaya and having just arrived back, was totally unaware of the family rift that had developed in his absence. It was pure luck that he had picked a time to call when my mam was out. My dad allowed him in and they exchanged pleasantries, but he was really there to see me. Here you are Alfie, he said, this is for you, and presented me with this huge parcel. He now had a smile that stretched from one ear to the other, making his nostrils flare and his thatch of jet black nasal hair protrude even more than it usually did. This being a dominant feature of a face that could otherwise be described as boyish. It was blatantly obvious that he had been looking forward to this moment ever since the day he'd bought it and was probably even more excited than I was at the prospect of what was inside. It was as big as a large shoebox and trembling with excitement I struggled to undo the string, -no cello-tape in those days - he produced a knife and cut through it. Throwing aside the brown paper wrapping, I was soon confronted by the most amazing toy that I had ever seen. It was a replica of a British army tank. Made of some sort of cast metal it had proper metal tracks and a turret that fired sparks, it also had the ability to change direction when confronted by an obstacle. I'm immediately thinking what reaction I'd get from school, surely none of my mates could possibly have seen anything like this, after all, this had come all the way from Malaya. My Uncle got his reward of a kiss and a hug from me and was rapidly shown the door by my nervous dad, whilst I was dispatched to bed, along with my tank of course.

Looking back on that day, it was quite obvious that my dad wanted to conclude matters quickly and get his brother away from the house before my mam got back. It must have been something of an anticlimax for him, having carried this present half way across the world he must have wished that he could have stayed a little longer to watch me play with it. My dad knew that if she discovered that he'd actually invited his brother into the house behind her back – as she saw it - the shit was bound to hit the proverbial fan. He also knew that he was just buying time because she was bound to find out in the morning.

He was off the hook for now, with me tucked up in bed along with the evidence, and he must have thought he'd be safely at work by the time I got up the next day.

Extremely excited and anxious to show off my new toy to my friends, I was up with the lark, and my tank of course. In fact, I was up so early that my dad had not yet left for work and mam was in the kitchen preparing his pack up lunch. "mam, look what uncle Brian's bought for me!" I could never have believed that this one simple sentence, uttered in all innocence then, would lead to such an explosion of hostility. As she launched a relentless verbal and physical attack on my dad, throwing whatever came to hand, I saw him cry. I knew there was no doubt, this was my fault, and I was absolutely terrified at the thought that it would be my turn next. On hearing the front door slam shut, as my dad made good his escape to the sanctuary of work, an eerie silence fell over the house and I wet myself as I awaited my fate. Tearfully clutching my tank and still in my wet pants, for the entire estate to see, I was dragged by my mother, out into the street around the corner to my grandma's house, to confront my very shocked uncle Brian. After loads more screaming and shouting she made me hand back my tank to him but he refused to take it. Eventually, she ripped it from my trembling grasp and threw it towards him, smashing it to the ground, I was then dragged by the opposite arm back home. There it was my sister Sue who gave me a hug and sorted out some dry clothes for me. I was inconsolable.

Seven

MY SECOND SCHOOL

I'm now off to my new school in my new outfit and I am not looking forward to it. Although it doesn't turn out to be as traumatic as I thought it might be, after all most of my friends from Bendbow rise infant school would be coming with me. Cort Crescent junior school was going to take care of my education for the next three years until I reached eleven years old. The school buildings were built just before the war and being mostly timber built were in urgent need of some repair. The teachers seemed, at first glance, to be extremely strict, or maybe this just appeared to be the case as it was my first encounter with the real world of education. Whatever it was about this school, I didn't like it very much!

My best mate at that time was Barry and he liked it even less than I did, and was in trouble with the teachers right from day one. Barry was a smashing lad but had a face that always had a blank, gormless looking expression. His jaw always hung open, prompting the teacher to ask if he was catching flies. It was this vacant look that ended with him suffering from a cut lip, after the teacher, Miss Brown, a menopausal lady in her mid forties who, would burst into tears any time at all and for no apparent reason, threw the blackboard duster at him hitting him squarely in the mouth. I think, amidst all the kids Mickey taking at her tears, she'd seen Barry as an easy target. I believe the excuse for the attack was that she thought he was pulling faces at her. I wonder what the implications of this attack would be in today's over protective society?

For recreation the school actively promoted boxing as the main sporting activity. All boys were expected to enter the boxing competitions, and the teachers were always encouraging us to join one competition or another. At the risk of sounding more than a little conceited, I reckoned I was quite good in the ring having had a great deal of early successes. But as with all boxers, I met my match on a couple of occasions, being totally out boxed each time. We were allowed to box for three rounds of a couple of minutes each and it was an all out brawl from the bell in order to end the fight quickly. Teachers were very careful not to allow a fight to carry on if a boy showed any signs of suffering. I am not sure what the weight of the gloves were but my God they became very heavy after three rounds. Only the strongest kids could lift them to protect themselves after more than two rounds and unfortunately I was not one of those select few. Surprisingly, with all this violence going on in the ring, to my knowledge it was never replicated in the playground, where bullying, as we know it today, was almost unheard of.

As far as I can remember there were no outdoor sports to talk of, as the school didn't have the facilities or the equipment for games such as football or rugby, although I do remember being taken by bus once a week to the local swimming baths. This was an ideal opportunity to have a bath, albeit without soap but also without all the tedious preparations I would have to go through at home.

I have one lasting memory about these trips to the baths, and this was the awful swimming trunks we used to have to wear. They were made of 100% wool and would smell terrible as soon as they got wet, we must have smelt like a field full of rain soaked sheep. They also became extremely baggy, hanging down to below our knees, leaving all our tackle hanging out for the entire world and his mum to see. Not that there was a great deal to see at that age, but it was still very embarrassing. Thinking back, we must have looked proper prats, extra's for the film "Gandhi" would have been a good description, as we trouped single file around the pool to the changing rooms.

Another humiliating memory I have of this school, was of performing a dance for one of the Christmas productions. The dance we did was to the "Trish trash Polka" and rehearsals went on for several weeks. It wasn't until just days before the performance was due to be presented, that we were given any idea what the costumes would be. Had I known I would most probably have feigned illness. The outfit consisted of a bright red leotard, which was to be worn under red shorts; the bottoms of which were to be tucked up inside the leotard. I looked an absolute Muppet! Since all the rest of the school, including parents would see this show, we were all more than a little concerned, to say the least, about what would happen to our street cred. This shouldn't happen to any boy, especially one who lives on the Braunstone estate. Nevertheless the show went ahead, and I pranced around as instructed, amazingly without any noticeable repercussions, or photos either, thankfully.

During my years at this school my parents decided that I would go home at lunchtime, as I lived quite nearby, rather than have school meals. I never fully understood the logic in this because I would have been entitled to free meals anyway because my parents were on benefits. Lunch at home could be anything from a bowl of cornflakes or semolina to a couple of slices of toast, depending on the funds available, on very rare occasions we would have a hot meal. This would consist of predominantly mashed potatoes, which was usually complemented by a slice of spam and tinned peas. Slight changes were made now and then when the spam was replaced with either a quarter of an individual steak and kidney pie, or one and a half skinless sausages. One of the dishes that I really made me heave, was a tin of vegetable soup poured over a plate of mashed potatoes accompanied by baked beans, but the worst of all was a couple of rashers of streaky bacon along with mashed potatoes and peas. This doesn't sound too bad until you consider that the bacon was fried in a pan a quarter full of lard with the remaining fat poured over the potatoes as a substitute for gravy. Cabbage sometimes substituted the peas in this revolting dish. Not surprisingly I developed a stomach ulcer in my early twenties.

My dad's meal was often very different from ours. For instance he would have a whole individual pie all to himself or, if he was in mam's good books, he would get a little lamb chop and a couple of proper sausages as I used to call them.

tea from a jam jar   *Alfie Watson*

These were the big fat ones with skins on. He would sometimes bring home some cheap meat from a butcher in the city centre market, supposedly to help with the family budget. But most often it would be for his personal consumption. He would buy things like pork belly or tripe, and occasionally he would buy the half of a pig's head he was so fond of, which he would devour within a couple of days of cooking it. I have to admit that the aroma as it was cooking was, to me, out of this world. It seemed that the fattier the meat was, the more he would enjoy it, a fact that would prove to have a profound effect on his health in later life. He would occasionally come home from work at lunchtime as well, that's assuming he had a job that week - and invariably would get into an argument with my mam. These fights were almost always about 'cigarettes' or should I say the lack of them, that being the reason for him coming home in the first place. It seemed he was being rationed to ten in the workday and another pack of ten for the evenings, but he could never make them last him. She had more hidden around the house but would steadfastly refuse to tell him where they were. Not being a smoker herself, she was quite ignorant to the fact that he was suffering from nicotine withdrawal symptoms and she had no compassion whatsoever for him.

This, not surprisingly put him in a lousy mood for the rest of the day and he'd arrive home from work in the evening, gasping for a fag. Woe betides me if I'd transgressed on one of those days!

Eight

THE GIGGLES

Weekend lunches were very different. If we had meat, and again, that depended on whether or not dad was working, it would usually be a leg of lamb. Mostly this would have been imported from New Zealand and the leg was one of the cheapest cuts available. There was quite a lot of fat on this joint which certainly suited my dad. Sunday was the one-day when we all sat down together. All seven of us and mam and dad, yes seven! The family actually numbered eight, the latest to appear was Mary and it wouldn't be long before she would need a space at the table too. These mealtimes were an absolute fiasco, with five of us squeezed around the small dining room table; there was no room for my sister Sue or myself. We would have to eat ours sitting on the staircase on these occasions, often eating from an upturned saucepan lid which served as a makeshift plate. These proved to be very practicable, as they were deeper than a plate so the risk of spillage was greatly reduced. Mam and dad would always eat theirs seated in their armchairs. There were never ever enough knives and forks to go round, so the younger ones had their food chopped up for them, and were given a spoon to eat it with. Sometimes, even then, for some reason there wouldn't be enough cutlery for everybody, so someone would have to finish before Sue or myself was able to eat ours. This often started an argument. I would be encouraging my younger brothers to hurry up, but typically this just made them eat even slower. Constantly reminding me that dad had told them to 'chew each mouthful thoroughly' before swallowing.

A favourite trick of dads was to forbid any of us to eat our meat, what little we had, until all signs of vegetables had disappeared from the plate. By which time we were all too full to want the meat anyway, he'd then scrape it all onto his plate and gorge himself until he was unable to move from his chair – not that he did that very often anyway- and within about half an hour he would be fast asleep, snoring like the pig he was! As can probably be guessed, I didn't care much for my dad and I'm absolutely sure the feeling was mutual.

One of these mealtimes holds particular memories for me. The meal had begun peacefully enough and I had somehow managed to get a seat at the table. Meal times for the majority of families was a time to chat about what kind of a day they'd each had, but not so in the Watson household, we had always been discouraged from speaking at the table, so meal times could be very tense affairs. Communication was done solely with eye contact. Sue was a very beautiful looking girl even at twelve, but she had this talent for making me laugh with just the slightest facial movement, always out of dad's view. I'd start to giggle and Horace would follow - and he really did have an infectious laugh - and one by one we all joined in. With the whole table reduced to the giggles, dad would initially become, irritated then annoyed then extremely angry, in the space of about five minutes. We knew from past experiences that we should stop now, or else! Try as we might we couldn't, by this time most of us wouldn't even know why we were laughing anyway. After leaving the room several times to compose myself, I'd find that as soon as I walked back in I'd start up again. My ribs were aching and my eyes were streaming and I'd also dribbled in my pants, but however much I tried, I couldn't stop. It was at this point that I parted company with half of one of my front teeth, as my dad decided that he'd had enough of all this joviality and smashed me in the mouth with a cycle lamp, this being the nearest heavy object at hand. A cushion would not have had the same effect.

The giggling stopped instantly, as I left the room, heading for the kitchen with my mouth bleeding profusely. I was screaming with severe pain, the worst pain I had known. I stood at the sink for quite some time washing away the endless flow of blood but it would not stop. The sharp point of the broken tooth had penetrated my upper lip and it was already very swollen. As I stood there alone - because no one was allowed to help me - it occurred to me that, I might possibly need some help with this; the bleeding just would not stop. I remember thinking that perhaps my dad hadn't realised how badly I had been hurt and that maybe once he saw it, he would show some guilt or remorse and help me. But he didn't want to see it because as soon as he heard the front room door handle turning as I tried to enter back into the room, he yelled at me to get out. I managed to control the bleeding eventually but the pain from the broken tooth was incessant. Neither of

tea from a jam jar *Alfie Watson*

my parents ever mentioned the matter again, not even to apologise and I never found the other half of my tooth either

In these early days friends were most important to me. I had met my best mate Barry a few years earlier when I had been living with my gran, as he was our next-door neighbour then. We used to go everywhere together; we'd spend endless hours playing on the grass outside his house. We'd play cricket, we'd wrestle, we'd do all the usual things normal kids did, and more.

A new fad was just becoming popular on the estate that would eventually become all the rage. I think we called this game simply " arrows". This involved the use of a modified standard dart. This would have to have the flight and stem taken out and replaced with a piece of cane about 12 inches long. This cane would have a small groove cut into it across the end. A piece of string of about 2 foot in length would be joined to make a complete loop, this was used in a sling fashion by hooking one end of the loop over the groove in the end of the stem, the other end of the loop was hooked around the index finger. Finger and thumb would now hold the barrel of the dart, which would then be shot, into the air in a normal throwing motion, with the string providing extra propulsion. These arrows provided hours of entertainment for all the local kids, with them reaching tremendous heights but as with most improvised kids' games, they often carried hidden dangers, and these darts would prove to be no exception. Hand Avenue, being grassed on both sides provided an ideal place to throw the arrows with both sides of the road occupied by around half a dozen lads throwing these things into the air and gazing skywards to watch the trajectory. This soon developed into a competition to see who could throw them the farthest and highest. With so many kids playing, it was difficult to keep a check on who was throwing what and It wasn't long before an accident happened.

One boy named Michael Collins had evidently just launched his missile and was watching its flight, when a dart thrown from the opposite direction, pierced his eye. What the odds would have been on such an accident happening, I'm not sure but it seemed to me at the time that he was extremely unlucky We found out later that he had lost his eye and was very fortunate not to have lost his life. That incident brought an abrupt end to this popular game, with all parents confiscating the arrows immediately.

Whip and top was another game that often ended suddenly, usually with the sound of breaking glass, as someone somehow managed to whip the top straight through a window and that someone was often me. I could never quite get the hang of these things. There were various shapes and sizes of tops but the only one I had a modicum of success with was the one resembling a large wooden tack. All the kids would decorate them with coloured chalk, which, if whipped and spun fast enough, looked like a Catherine wheel of sorts. Most kids would for some reason, tie a knot in the end of the whips lace or leather. This was apparently supposed to get the top spinning even faster. Well it didn't work for me, all that served to do was send the top higher into the air.

Other games, often with very strange names, like tick, jarlesio, tin lurky and regular ones like hopscotch, football, rounder's, hide and seek, would be played out in cul-de-sacs or pudding bags, as we used to call them, all over the estate.

When darkness fell, an air of devilment would automatically take over Barry and me. If some neighbours were unhappy with our daytime pranks, and there was a few, then they were about to be driven to despair by our night time ones. These would include all those usual childish tricks like knocking doors, and throwing pebbles at windows and legging it. We invented a more sophisticated game - well we thought we had - that was absolutely guaranteed to drive the locals crazy but would also ensure that we were far enough away, not to be implicated, when the trap was sprung. This new form of entertainment involved the use of one or two empty milk bottles, which could always be found at the side of every doorstep at night, and several yards of fishing line or strong cotton. We would tie the necks of the bottles carefully together on a doorstep, and then repeat this at the house directly opposite on the other side of the road. A length of line would join the two target houses together. With the line stretched across the road it was time to hide and await the arrival of some unsuspecting driver, usually the L2 Midland red bus, which would hit the line and deliver the coup de grace, smashing the bottles on both sides of the road simultaneously and making an almighty din. The pair of us would be lying in lord knows what! under someone's hedge absolutely wetting ourselves in hysterical yet muffled laughter, while the occupants could be heard yelling threats and warnings at the unseen perpetrators. Great fun!

Another prank, which we often used to great effect, also involved the use of fishing line or catgut. A smallish parcel, about the size of cigarette packet, would be wrapped very neatly and connected to the line; it would then be left in the shadows of a street light. We would then hide and wait patiently in a nearby garden, usually well concealed under a privet hedge, which in those days every house seemed to grow. Sometimes the wait would seem endless but we would be in fits of giggles just imagining what was about to happen or how the previous snare had been sprung. At the uppermost end of Bendbow Rise and close to my first school, sat the Braunstone Victoria Working Men's Club, which provided most of our victims. They would stagger their way home chattering some strange gibberish, which only they could understand. Our strategically placed parcel would soon attract their attention, amazingly even if they were on the opposite side of the road, predictably one of them would spot the package and stagger across to pick it up. A sharp tug on the line would send them running as fast as their wobbly legs could safely carry them. On some occasions when groups of them would be lured into our trap, it often ended with the woman or women in the group, screaming hysterically, with Barry and me being hotly pursued by the irate husbands or boyfriends.

Because the lamp post we were using was on the corner right next to my house, the noise soon brought our activities

tea from a jam jar   *Alfie Watson*

to the attention of my dad, who as usual wasted no time at all in connecting with the part of my anatomy he seemed to dislike the most, my face, or to be more accurate, the side of my head. He was absolutely right to stop us because we hadn't considered the implications of what we were doing. In just the same way that my dad's penchant for whacking me over my ears would result in a perforated eardrum, these antics could quite easily have resulted in anyone of these people having a heart attack. Once behind closed doors the leather belt was put to use. After my beating it was usual for me to be kept in for maybe a week or more, [grounded].

As I was the eldest boy, I had certain daily duties to perform, none of which I particularly liked. One of these was emptying the poe. The poe or piss pot, as some people called it, was in fact a chamber pot, which used to sit on the landing at the top of the stairs and was there for night-time toiletry needs. It fell to me to empty it each and every morning. It was placed there on the understanding that it should only be used for number 'ones', but it was not unusual to find that someone had left a little extra. Each morning, with arms outstretched, the night's takings were cautiously carried down the thirteen or so stairs, with each step upsetting my balance enough to cause the contents to slop over my hands and the staircase below, through the kitchen to the outside toilet. The overwhelming smell of ammonia was quite revolting, and could be smelt all over the house for some time. This was now my most hated chore, relegating pumping water to the bath into second place by a mile.

tea from a jam jar *Alfie Watson*

It wasn't difficult to find out which households used a poe at night. A glance up at the living room ceiling in any house on the estate would give a clue; there would most definitely be a large brown stain. This was largely due to the fact that the poe had continued to be used even when it was full. Also, with it being such a small target and with no light available, some users, especially the boys, would miss it altogether. Consequently there would be an overflow onto the landing floor and eventually through to the ceiling.

After this chore was completed, the next task was to light the fire in the living room. First the grate had to be cleaned out, and the ashes thrown onto the garden. Apparently it was supposed to help break down the soil. Newspaper rolled up tightly, formed the basis for the new fire, this was followed by a few bits of firewood and coke. Coke -coal with all of the gas taken out - was a cheap and plentiful fuel, which was smokeless, a requirement that had recently become law. Ignition of the fire was by way of more rolled up newspaper, which had to be lit on the kitchen stove and carried hurriedly through the hall into the living room to the fire grate. Then came the fun. In order to get the coke to burn, it would need a little encouragement by way of a dustbin lid and a sheet or two of newspaper, the News of the World being the preferred one because it was big enough to cover the bin with one sheet. The dustbin lid was placed across the front of the fire and the newspaper put over the top of it. An outside door would be opened in order to create a draught, usually the back door. Within seconds the fire could be heard roaring as the flames were dragged up the chimney. Very soon and with little or no warning, the paper would start to scorch, meaning that the essence of the next part of the operation was definitely one of speed, because it was at this point that the newspaper had to be removed before it caught alight. I was more than often a bit too slow, and could regularly be seen running from the house via the front door, with it ablaze in my hands leaving bits of charred and burning paper floating into the room behind me. All this was conducted in full view of my younger siblings without an adult in sight. In view of my previous involvement with matches, it seemed incredible to me and neglectful of my parents, that I was allowed to perform this task at all.

When the stock of coke needed replenishing it would also fall to me to fetch it. Who needs slaves when you've got kids? The coal wharf was situated about half a mile away, just behind my school, and I was a frequent visitor there during the winter months. Arriving home from school and already frozen to the bone, I would immediately be dispatched, along with an old pram, to fetch, usually, a quarter but sometimes half of a hundred weight of coke, which was 14lbs and 28 lbs. Such an amount barely lasted more than two days, hence the reason I was such a regular visitor. The wharf occupied a small piece of land between two houses the area being probably just about large enough to build another property on. One strategically placed lamp gave it an eerie look and hardly provided enough light to see anything, especially the scales. A set of large black cast iron balance scales were used to weigh the coke, with one man shovelling it into the sack while another blocked the view of the scales. So trust was the order of the day. There would always be an enormous queue of kids there and it was always extremely cold. There was a connection there – the cold and the queue –and this was because many families were living on the bread line, and a fire was seen as rather a luxury and considered to be literally like "pushing money up the chimney" as my parents often said. A bout of severe cold weather would leave them with little choice but to light one. Hence the mad rush for fuel. I have stood in that queue, still in just my school clothes, with my toes so cold that it felt as if my shoes were frozen to my feet. My shoes were worn so badly that holes had appeared in the soles. Even before the holes had appeared they were so thin that they gave little or no protection. A piece of cardboard inserted into the shoe provided the only barrier from the elements. Sometimes I wouldn't have any "proper" shoes to wear, only canvass plimsolls. I would stand there trembling from head to foot, breathing through my nose because to do so through my mouth would set my broken tooth off again.

Arriving back home extremely cold wet and hungry. Priority and it has to be said, some pity was shown to me on these occasions, and I was allowed closest to the fire, that is until, "hot aches" took over when I would quickly retreat to the back of the room. I could never understand why it proved more painful to get warm than it was to get cold.

The long dark winters seemed endless back then and certainly felt colder. Frosts during these months seemed a

tea from a jam jar   *Alfie Watson*

daily occurrence and if it wasn't frosty it would be snowing or sleeting. Many happy hours could be spent making slides on the frozen pavements, some reaching fifteen to twenty feet in length. Provided you had leather-soled shoes, and I didn't, great speeds could be achieved. These slides would pop up all around the estate especially on hills and would last for several days, until some spoilsport parent put salt or ashes on it, usually as a result of a complaint from an elderly pedestrian.

Nine

THE TELLY

The day the television arrived at my grandma and granddad's house was around 1954-55 and was an enormously big event. Looking back on those day's I can't help wondering why on earth they spent what must have been an awful lot of money on a television, when the house could politely be described as, in need of a makeover!!

Word soon got around whenever a new set appeared on the estate and this was no different. This little box with its 12-inch screen set into a three or four foot high cabinet was soon the talk of the entire street. And I admit to having a small part to play in spreading the news. When my grandma was in a really good mood she'd let us in for a while. I cant remember what sort of programmes we watched but the room was full of my friends, the small ones sitting on the floor at the front while the others sat behind them, often on chairs brought with them to ensure they could watch in comfort. Some who weren't so lucky, tried to get a glimpse through the window. It was such a spectacle that I remember watching in awe and wondering how on earth such things were possible. The programmes were transmitted in black and white, although I always thought brown and white would have been a better description. My grandma actively encouraged me to visit whenever I wanted; but I'd always make sure my mam didn't get to know about it. As far as I was concerned I didn't care less what they got to find out but I'd keep it a secret to protect my grandma.

Ten

TROLLY RACES

As winter gave way to spring and then summer a new craze was beginning to sweep the estate. All kids throughout history have needed a craze or obsession. No sooner had one had ended, another would start up! Trolley racing was now growing fast, and all the boys on the estate were busy building their own models with whatever parts they could find. The wheels were usually taken from disused prams and because of the demand, they were hard to come by. It didn't matter what size of wheel we used as long as we had two the same, usually ending up with a pair of quite large ones for the back and two small ones for the front. There was talk of prams being stolen just for their wheels! The axles were fixed to a piece of timber, which was around three feet long. This in turn had to be fixed securely to the main body with nails. The body came in all shapes and sizes, depending on what sort of materials were around. Often though this would just be a plank of wood around five feet long. The front wheels for steering were fitted, like the rear, to a piece of wood and connected to the body by a bolt or large nail. A length of rope or electrical cable was fixed, again by nails, to each side of the front wheels to provide the steering. This was used only when the trolley was being driven in the sitting position. The most common way to ride these things was to lay flat on your stomach with your hands doing the steering by gripping the front axle, providing much better aerodynamics, and therefore greater speeds.

My mate Barry had a trolley to beat all trolleys. His had a steering wheel and proper brakes including a hand brake. His dad was an engineer and had helped him build it. Although it was state of the art, it wasn't all that fast, because he always had to sit upright in order to steer.

Just as with other childhood games I've mentioned trolley racing tended to become very competitive and races soon began to take place on many downhill stretches on the estate. In our area, the track that we used stretched the complete length of Bendbow Rise, from the very top of the hill to the very bottom and sometimes further, probably around six or seven hundred yards. This would necessitate the crossing of two quite major roads, and also, five junctions! Three or four trolleys would race at a time; some of them would be carrying passengers. This would be achieved by the passenger usually lying on top of the driver, a very precarious position to be in, especially when taking corners. The starting line was outside the working men's club at the top of the hill and a push from a mate would ensure that we all got a good start. After maybe two or three hundred yards we were confronted with a sharp left, almost hairpin bend, that led straight onto the first busy road. There were no brakes on these contraptions, unless your name was Barry, so slowing down was achieved by dragging the toes of your shoes on the road. It was at this stage of the track that most of the accidents happened, with trolleys overturning or crashing into each other, with passengers rolling off onto the road. If you were lucky or skilled enough to negotiate this, then the next bend, a right-hander, was just a matter of a few feet away. A straight run of a hundred yards now before another left or right turn, either side of the old oak tree, depending on your choice, - although quite often there wasn't one, you just had to go with the flow - then a long fast stretch down to the next major road and the finish line.

It wasn't unusual for one of us to end the day sitting in the casualty department of the Leicester Royal Infirmary. My turn came one fateful evening on the first bend, near to the top of the hill, when I got involved in a pile up. During the smash I had somehow caught my leg on a bent rusty nail that was used to secure the wheel to the rear axle, gashing my thigh quite badly. Several hours and many stitches later I arrived home to face the fury of my, unusually concerned dad. Predictably, the end result was a total ban on trolley racing for me. While I can appreciate that the roads were not as busy then, it still remains a mystery to me why no one was either killed or seriously injured.

One boy who used to hang around with us was always tempting fate whatever he did. Danny Clarke was his name. If Danny rode a bike he'd have his feet on the handlebars or he'd be standing on the crossbar while holding on to the handlebars. If the rest of us were to get from a 10ft high roof we'd probably hang by our fingertips to reduce the height of the drop. Not Danny, he'd jump the full distance. We swore he was made of rubber. Climbing trees was his speciality. He

tea from a jam jar — Alfie Watson

always headed for the highest branches and would hang by his feet from what generally appeared to be the weakest of them all. This boy knew no fear; either that or he had a death wish. I've seen him fall when a branch he was hanging from at the top of a tree had broken and remarkably manage to grab hold of another on the way down. Then instead of climbing back down to the safety of the ground, he would go straight back to the top, as if to show he hadn't been beaten. He was a strange lad, and a bit of a loner. He could often be found at the roadside, struggling with all his might, to lift up a storm drain cover, so he could dredge the bottom in search of, who knows what? I don't know if he ever found anything of value, but I do know that on one occasion he came to a very sticky end. The lids to these drains were about six inches thick and extremely heavy. They were hinged for easy access, and Council workers, always opened them fully, first to the upright position and then with a kick they would send them crashing to the floor. This meant that the lid was laying flat to the road, with no risk of it falling while work was carried out. Although he was very strong for his age, Danny only lifted the lids to an upright position, thus when he'd finished he could just tap it with his toe and it would be closed again with a loud crash. It was one of these cast covers that was to put him in hospital for a long time. The story goes that he had just hauled himself out of the drain, were he used to hang head-first whilst searching through the slurry on the bottom. The lid had fallen from its precariously balanced position, trapping his right arm. Luckily he must have had something there, perhaps his coat or perhaps a piece of wood, that prevented the lid from completely closing, otherwise he would have definitely lost his arm. Somehow he managed to pull himself from underneath the lid, taking the skin and a good deal of muscle and flesh off the whole length of his crushed arm in the process.

Danny was taken to hospital in a critical condition mostly due to his loss of blood. After several transfusions and skin grafts and many weeks in hospital he was discharged. He was a year older and quite a bit wiser when I saw him again, with the most awful scars as a reminder for the rest of his life.

tea from a jam jar   *Alfie Watson*

Eleven

MY FIRST HOLIDAY

It may have been great timing on someone's part, or perhaps it was just coincidence but the local education authority were about to take me and many more underprivileged kids, away from all of this for a holiday in Mablethorpe. Provided and supported by the good people of Leicestershire, the Mablethorpe Children's Home, situated on the east coast, had provided traditional seaside holidays for poor and under privileged children aged 7 to 11 years old since its formation in 1898. The charity has provided holidays for more than 50.000 children, and continues to do so to this day. I was to be one of the lucky ones. Once I knew I was going and a date had been set, the days just couldn't pass quick enough.

Well! That day had now arrived when Alfie and his tatty little leather suitcase - packed with heaven knows what - headed into town with his mam and dad, to catch the coach for the trip of a lifetime. There we stood, trembling with excitement at the prospect of what lay ahead. Still not quite believing that we had been especially selected for this fortnight of over indulgence. Eventually after waiting for what seemed an eternity, the coach arrived. And after hugs, kisses and a few tears, we were soon bundled on board, and

tea from a jam jar   *Alfie Watson*

then with our parents waving anxiously their goodbyes, some not using all of their fingers, we were finally on our way. For all of us, this was to be our first holiday, the first time away from our parents, and for many, the first time we had seen the sea. The journey seemed to take hours, about three to be exact, we were expecting to see the sea after half an hour had past. Looking anxiously towards the horizon each time the coach emerged from a bend or reached the top of a hill.

When we did finally get there we were met by the staff who would be looking after us for the next two weeks. They all stood outside the main entrance, the matron and her husband, flanked by the cooks, waitresses and the maids, all resplendent in their various uniforms! One of the nicest recollections of my time there was the wealth of food, and the regularity at which it was served. There was breakfast, elevenses, then lunch, tea, and the one I looked forward to most of all, supper! Even now, when I think about those days, I can almost smell the hot chocolate and the bread and dripping, which was served to us every night before bedtime. That holiday in Mablethorpe turned out to be the happiest time of my young life. Children from both sexes shared all the facilities, but it was quite noticeable that we were kept apart whenever it was possible. The dining room was split in half with the boys on one side and the girls on the other. Obviously the sleeping arrangements were separate and took the form of dormitories, sleeping about twenty in each room. Days were spent playing games in the sand dunes and on the beach behind the home.

tea from a jam jar   *Alfie Watson*

Any money we had was taken from us when we'd arrived on the first day by the Matron who duly noted all the various amounts, then handed it back to us daily to spend at the local shops or on the small fun fair, which was conveniently sited yards from the home. If she hadn't done this, I feel sure most of us would have been skint after a couple of days, especially me. Needless to say my first letter home was to ask for more money, but it was never forthcoming.

One of the many friends I made during my stay there was a boy named Michael, a good looking lad who came from a children's home just a few miles outside Leicester. We continued our friendship for a short time on returning from Mablethorpe but I never did find out why he was there. I find it incredible that at the age of ten, I was allowed to travel alone to visit him often catching a train there and back. As long as I was home by eight o'clock, no questions would be asked. I couldn't help feeling fortunate after my visits. After all I'd got brothers and sisters to go home to, even though we hardly ever got on together. All Michael had was strangers to share his life with, in an extremely noisy home. Until then I never realised that such places as these existed. Why would any parent want to send their child to such an establishment? Suddenly my life wasn't so bad after all! One thing I noticed that Michael had - and I hadn't - was the use of a television, albeit a communal one. This had to be one of the greatest inventions of my childhood and had now slowly become available to the working classes.

Another friend I met at Mablethorpe, was Linda who came

from the other side of town from me. We'd spent a bit of time together in the sand dunes behind the home. Some kissing and fumbling took place and I was besotted by her. I was absolutely sure that this was love. It must have been because every time we kissed I got an erection, how could it be anything else? I went to visit Linda when I returned home. Although she said she lived in Leicester, her home was miles away from mine. I made the trip a couple of times but it was two bus rides away and a few pennies more than I could afford. After a couple of visits you could say we drifted apart. So it wasn't love after all!!

Twelve

DETECTOR VANS

We got our own television set around 1956, when picture quality had improved considerably and the screen size was now a massive 14 inch. The set was rented, and a shilling (5 new pence) had to be inserted into a slot at the back. This would probably provide a couple of hours viewing. At the weekend the rental company sent someone to empty the box on the back of the set and our parents were given the balance after the rent had been deducted, thus leaving us with a few shillings for more viewing time. The very first programmes I can remember were "emergency ward 10" and "Lunch box" with Noel Gordon later to star in "Crossroads".

People on the estate could barely raise the money to rent a television, so when they did; they were not about to part with more to buy a license. So to track down these 'license dodgers', the government let the detector vans loose on them. It really didn't need such a sophisticated van, loaded with high tech. surveillance equipment to find them; the aerial was a dead give-away. When news spread around the estate that the detector vans were in the area, television sets would begin to vanish. Some folk would hide them in the coal-house; some thought it would be safer in the rabbit hutch, or in the attic. Some families such as ours would load the set into a pram or wheelbarrow, ours being the old wooden coal barrow, and take it to friend or relatives house, who already had a licence, for safe keeping. Without the proof of actually having a receiver – the technical name for a TV –there could be no prosecution. This often meant that we could spend days without the 'magic box' until the heat was off, when normality would be restored once more, until that is, that damned detector van would turn up again.

Thirteen

SEX INSTRUCTION

The rabbit hutch was also to provide the props when, my dad, in his wisdom, decided to explain the facts of life. The lecture began with my dad, holding by the ears, a buck rabbit in one hand and a doe in the other. After explaining which was which he placed them down and started to show me with his fingers how procreation took place. With his left hand he created a hole, using the index finger to touch the tip of his thumb to represent the female genitals; a stiff index finger on his right hand was the penis. He then started to demonstrate by pushing the finger in and out of his left hand, thus demonstrating copulation! The duration of this "lesson" was accompanied by his unintelligible instruction, and my input of 'I know dad' 'I know.' Well, that was it, the whole of my parental sex education over in less than a couple of minutes. Still, at least he made an attempt to explain, some of my mates were never told at all. He certainly devoted more time and effort explaining and trying to demonstrate the facts of life to one of my sisters. At least that's what he said he was doing as I disturbed him one day.

In those days I used to run everywhere, no matter where I was going, it could be to the shops, round my mate's house or just upstairs, I was always in a hurry. So it wasn't surprising that I arrived at the top of the stairs without warning, to witness him with my sister pinned against the wall trying to kiss and grope her. She was struggling to untangle herself from him and pleading for him to leave her alone. My arrival startled him and she made good her getaway to the relative safety of her bedroom and slammed the door shut behind her. I was to observe a similar encounter, also with the same sister, some time later in my parent's bedroom. To this day these two incidents have never been discussed.

It's now the Easter holidays, and all-good things must come to an end, as they say, it was time to concentrate on exams. We would soon be sitting the eleven plus, a process designed to determine our next school. Pass and I would be off to Grammar school and a better standard of education. Failure meant me ending up in a Secondary Modern, "secondary" being a very appropriate choice of word.

There was pandemonium as dawn broke at 43 Bendbow Rise that August morning in 1956. It was back to school, and for some of us that meant a completely fresh start, with new teacher's, new friends and a complete change of environment. I wasn't particularly looking forward to this day with much relish. A lot had been rumoured about how tough it was going to be when we moved up. Having left my old school some seven or eight weeks previous, where we had enjoyed a whole final term as the seniors, commanding respect from all the other kids, we were now about to find out how it felt to be the new boys or juniors again. Barry would not be coming with me and I knew I was going to miss him quite a lot. No, he hadn't gone on to a Grammar school! He lived just inside a different catchment area and he would be sent to Wycliffe Secondary School, along with many more of my friends. During the summer break I had been kitted out with the necessary school uniform, courtesy of the local education authority as with my previous school, because my parents were still unable to afford them. The uniform consisted of grey trousers, black blazer, emblazoned with the school badge, grey shirt with a blue and white diagonal striped tie and brightly polished black shoes.

The first day passed without incident, as everyone was kept busy being categorised and sorted into the various forms or classes. During the breaks or play times, it became quite obvious to me that the fourth year boys were going to be a problem to us young uns before long. Some of these lads were as big, if not bigger than many of the teachers. From these had been selected the school prefects, in my opinion another word for bullies. It seemed strange to me that even the teachers seemed bigger than at my last school. I have to admit that it was clear after that first day that it was not going to be an easy ride. Totally new subjects were going to be introduced, such as woodworking, metalwork, and gardening. The latter was to become my favourite lesson.

At approximately the same time as starting at Ellesmere school I had landed a job at one of the local grocery shops. I was employed as a delivery boy but my duties included helping out in the shop, which I did when there was no deliveries. I was the only male along with three females one of which was the boss, Miss Shipman. Many items that she sold were delivered to the store in a loose or bulk state and these had to be weighed or measured as the customer requested. Miss Shipman was an extremely accommodating and understanding lady, she knew, often first hand, the hardships her customers had to contend with and nothing was too much trouble for her. She would always accommodate her customers whenever she could. For instance she would sell half a loaf or a quarter of a pound of sugar. Lard, margarine, tea, flour, rice, practically anything she could split she would, that included cigarettes. One other commodity that required splitting or measuring was left solely for me to deal with and this was the vinegar from the barrel. The barrel was kept in the yard and during the summer months it would be swarming with wasps. Customers would bring in a variety of bottles to be filled, sometimes milk or sauce bottles. I kept a funnel inside the shop, away from the wasps which I would place in the neck of the bottle before venturing outside, and then, in one swift movement I would open the tap and at the same time place the bottle and funnel under it, then leg it to safety until it was full. That was the only job I can honestly say I disliked whilst working there , yet amazingly I cannot remember ever being stung.

This shop job brought me many new friends, some good ones and many that were not so good. This was the time in my life when it was considered macho to try some forbidden fruits; like sex and cigarettes for example. The latter of these was the one that these undesirable friends were mostly interested in. My working hours, if I can remember correctly,

tea from a jam jar   *Alfie Watson*

were from five o'clock in the evening until six and then all day Saturday. They would come into the shop on the pretext of perhaps to buy just a loaf of bread, for instance. As soon as Miss Shipman's attention was distracted they would indicate with two fingers holding an imaginary cigarette or fag, as we called them, just what they really wanted. These lads meant business and were not going to take no for an answer. As the loaf was handed over it was invariably accompanied by twenty fags. It was not difficult to deceive Miss Shipman, she was very trusting and, I'm sad to say very naive. But my antics soon came to the notice of another member of the shop staff who warned me that she had observed what was happening and unless it "stopped right now" she would inform Miss Shipman.

This lady was Mrs Price, a lovely cheery lady who I bonded with on my first day there. She was the one who put her arms around me within minutes of me arriving and said "lets put the kettle on, shall we?" She explained that she was in full charge when Miss Shipman was absent, which, she says was not very often. She would spend her time in the shop weighing out the products into individual bags or packs whilst Miss Shipman and the other lady who I have yet to mention, Beryl, would help in the shop, serving the customers Whilst her threats to report me were meant to be taken seriously, she was also aware of the predicament I was in and because of this allowed things to carry on longer than she would normally have done. By the time my final ultimatum was given, I was stealing fags in boxes of 200 at a time.

Something had to be done, and soon!

Some of the booty was for my own use; I had started to smoke almost as soon as I moved up to Ellesmere, where everybody did it. I had always been curious about smoking since watching my dad when I was a kid. Watching him blow smoke down his nose, had a particular fascination for me. I think I must have been about ten years old when I had my first puff. This was from a stub that I'd taken from his ashtray in the bedroom. Straightened out it measured about half an inch long, and the strongest part of a fag, I was to be informed later. Immediately after lighting up I had blown the smoke through my nose, just like dad did, only I hadn't inhaled first. The awful dizzy, sick feeling that flooded over me would put me off doing it again for a very long time, but sadly not for ever.

I had to tell the boys that I had been supplying, that the party was now over and that the owner had caught me and threatened me with the sack. Luckily they accepted it quite well initially. But, like any drug addict, these boys had to have their "fix." They were well and truly hooked and could not exist without them. I was now under such pressure to supply them that new ways had to be found to get them from the shop.

Most grocery deliveries would take place towards the end of the week and while packing them into the boxes I would slip in a couple of packets of fags. These fags would be handed over to the thugs who were loitering just around the corner. It soon became clear to me that I was never going to satisfy their demands so I made the decision to stop. It didn't go down too well at first and I suffered quite a bit of grief from some of them, a lot of which went on for many months . I would often meet up with my old mate Barry after school, that used to help, his size would present something of a deterrent to anybody. Barry was always a big lad, even at junior school but he had really grown since moving up. He was a gentle giant really, but his presence almost always had the desired effect.

The fact they were not getting their fags was not the only reason I was getting grief from these people, many of whom were once my mates. Word had obviously got around about my dad's latest occupation. I don't know what must have been going through his head at the time but he had decided to become a policeman, well a "special constable" was the proper title. Talk about the enemy within. The estate thrived on corruption and wheeling and dealing, just the same as estates do today. So it was understandable that people would give anyone from our family a wide birth. As if life wasn't tough enough, what a prick!!

Now that I had made the decision to stop stealing from the shop, I couldn't support my own use any more and sometimes had to walk the couple of miles to school using the bus fare to buy a fag, often arriving late for school. I would always catch the bus home after school because to be late home would inevitably cause questions to be asked and I could definitely do without that.

tea from a jam jar   *Alfie Watson*

Buses in those days had no passenger doors, so when the bus was full, and at school chucking out time, it invariably was, the conductor hooked a leather strap across the platform in order to prevent more people getting on and to stop people falling off. These straps were often used by school kids, intent on causing mayhem. It was usual for us kids to jump off as the bus was slowing down. The challenge was always to see who'd have the balls to jump first, almost as soon as the driver had started to apply the brakes. On one particular day, as I jumped, one of these thugs hooked the strap into the pocket of my blazer, tearing the pocket and jacket beyond repair. Of course nobody knew who had done it; it could have been any one of about ten who were getting off at that stop. I had my own idea who was responsible. I knew straight away that this would not go down too well at home. I will be expecting the leather belt to be in use again tonight, when my dad gets home. The immediate reaction of my parents was that I should tell them who was responsible. Obviously I couldn't do that. So I was grounded for quite some time, meaning I couldn't work at the shop. If they were hoping that I would relent and spill the beans, then it could be a long wait. My mother decided that in the meantime, she would go to the school and speak to the Headmaster. All this achieved was for me to get a great deal of ridicule from the other boys which on occasions could be most embarrassing. News of anyone's mother coming to the school spread like wildfire, always with the same outcome. Now, because of her actions, the headmaster spoke about it at morning assembly, warning of the dangers of such pranks and naming me as the victim. I was now a target for all the kids, mainly the older ones, who, if they hadn't heard about my mothers visit, would be assuming that I had reported it directly to the headmaster. I did suffer for a while from the taunts but they passed with time. The culprit got his comeuppance a little while later. While he was playing rugby on the school playing fields, his clothes mysteriously disappeared from the changing rooms.

Time, as they say is a great healer and it soon became clear that the free riding thugs had realised that there was most definitely to be no more fags for them. Most of them had now left school anyway to start work, so I didn't see them that often. To think, these people were once considered to be my friends but I was amazed at how quickly I became their enemy when the freebies stopped.

I'm now a little older and becoming a little more streetwise, I'm also a member of one of the biggest gangs on the estate. When we all turned out, we were a formidable force. Now the dust had settled I started to steel a few fags again for my own use, but it was becoming more and more difficult as they were now kept more secure. I loved my job in the shop. I particularly liked it when I could slip a little something extra into poor pensioner's groceries, such as a cream cake or a packet of biscuits, as you may imagine I soon became very popular with them.

Fourteen

THE BULLET

Sport at this new school was actively promoted at every opportunity and my choice became rugby; a game that did not particularly suit my physique, but even so, I enjoyed it immensely. I think what appealed to me most was the team spirit that our sport teacher, Mr Hadden, had instilled into us. There was a great feeling of camaraderie, a feeling of belonging. I always enjoyed away games more as this gave me the chance to travel, even though it was only around the city. Saturday mornings were match days, and the afternoon was set aside for recovering.

I can remember quite clearly waking up at home on one particular Saturday afternoon to be told that I had been brought off after ten minutes with concussion and I had the lump to prove it. Kicked in the head during a scrummage, was the report I got from my team mates on arrival back at school on Monday. It was not unusual for me to be sporting a black eye or a cut or two. Battle scars I preferred to call them and I bore them with pride. While it was never my intention to deliberately get injuries, I didn't half have my fair share. Breaking my arm in two places playing football, fracturing my ankle when getting hit by the ball while playing cricket and suffered concussion many times playing rugby.

The one sporting activity that I managed to come through

tea from a jam jar *Alfie Watson*

unscathed was cross country running, in which I excelled, at one stage being selected to run against an all County line-up, although I can't remember the distance we ran but it was probably about 5-6 miles and I finished a credible 8th. This aptitude for running had probably been developed whilst making good my escape from one prank or another in previous years, although I did have the physical aptitude needed for this sport. Namely, long skinny legs! It was during a school run around the perimeter of Braunstone Park – a distance of about three miles – when myself and one or two others had ventured onto the park, without the knowledge of the teachers. The nissen huts that had been occupied by the American forces had now been demolished leaving behind an assortment of broken and damaged military machinery. It was as we were hunting through the rubbish, that I came across three live .202 rifle bullets. Now this really was a spectacular find, something that would definitely impress my mate's back at school. I had heard stories of people finding ammunition on the park before and had done my share of searching, always drawing a blank. I carried them around in my pocket for several days, before giving one of them to Barry.

After school one day I decided to see if it was possible to explode one of these shells, so a small group of us came up with the idea of throwing them at the tarmac pavement. We took turns to throw them as hard as possible at the floor, totally oblivious to the dangers of what we were doing. I remember being in such a rush to grab the bullet and have a throw that we were diving to the ground to pick it up before it had even landed. Because the shell had been thrown at the floor maybe a hundred or more times without result, we hadn't really expected anything to happen. Then suddenly "BANG" it went off and so did we. We left the scene at such speed, driven I suppose by sheer adrenalin and panic. We stopped some two or three hundred yards away, breathless and shaking with fear at the realisation of how lucky we were not to have been seriously injured. I don't know what happened to the remaining bullet, I suspect it was probably left lying on the footpath ready for some other kid to find.

After school I had to get in touch with Barry, to find out if he still had the one I'd given him about a week earlier. Luckily he still had it in his pocket but wasn't about to part with it, even after I'd told him about the lucky escape we'd had when ours went off. A few days later he'd had the idea of taking it into his dad's shed to try to fire it. Because his dad was an engineer there was no shortage of tools. He had clamped the bullet case into the vice that was fixed to the bench. With it facing the back wall of the shed he'd proceeded to create an improvised firing pin. This took the form of a hammer and a nail, when this had failed he used a steel punch and after several attempts it went off. Lucky for Barry, it must have turned slightly in the jaws of the vice and pierced a neat little hole in the roof of the shed.

What would have happened if it had not moved, but had gone through the back wall? It doesn't bear thinking about because immediately behind the shed were more houses and gardens, where possibly children could have been playing.

Fifteen

GARDENING

This proved to be by far my preferred subject. At this school we had our own greenhouses, where all manner of things were grown. We grew all the popular types of vegetables such as potatoes, cabbage, peas, carrots, cauliflower etc. These were sold to the locals at what must have been very reasonable prices, judging by the amount of customers we attracted. These sales took place outside the school gates twice a week. Flowers were also grown for sale and the ones I remember attracting the biggest queues were the Chrysanthemums and Dahlias, which were the favourite of our gardening teacher Mr Percy. Of course we also grew and sold spring and summer flowers and plants but these were the stars. They were meticulously cared for especially during the winter months when they would have to be kept safe from any frost. They'd be buried about a foot underground in the cold frames, in special compost – containing dried pigs blood - made by Mr Percy. It always seemed to me that they needed an awful lot of attention. But come late summer we realised they were well worth the effort. We produced the most gorgeous Blooms I've ever seen, with such huge flower heads worthy of a prize at any horticultural show. The unsold vegetables were given to the school kitchens. And I presume, any cash took at the school gate sales would be used by Mr

Percy to fund the running costs. I think it must have been due to the fact that each and every lesson was in the open, that drew me into gardening. I became to love the fresh air along with the lovely smells of the various fruits and vegetables. During rainy days our lessons would continue in one of the two large greenhouses where we were shown pricking out and transplanting procedures.

The highlight of the gardening calendar for me, was when we had to fetch manure from a disused sewage farm situated on the edge of the town. In one day we managed to load and unload two lorry loads of manure. This was in turn spread on the vegetable garden or laid in trenches, over the following Autumn and Winter months ready for potato planting.

The trip to the sewage farm, although exciting enough, brought an extra treat for all of us. Tomatoes grew in abundance and we picked them by the carrier bag full to take home. Until Mr Percy explained how the seed that had produce them had survived the journey through a human body only to grow again in raw sewage. Well we'd been eating them all afternoon and now he tells us.

tea from a jam jar　　　　　　　　　　　　　*Alfie Watson*

Sixteen

THE ARMY CADETS

It was around this time that we - Barry and me - joined the Army Cadets. A local school was used as the headquarters for C Company, as we were known. This school was about two mile away with classes attended one night a week. I remember really looking forward to these nights, when we would don our uniforms and march all the way there and then parade around the school playground whilst waiting for the class to start, much to the amusement of the local kids.

The top man of our group was Captain English, a small stocky little man who resembled Arthur Lowe's character in dads Army. He was very intimidating and extremely strict. His knowledge about the army knew no bounds but It was one thing to have all this knowledge and another to be able to pass it on to the likes of us. I always felt that he lacked the necessary teaching skills and this might explain why he got so frustrated with us sometimes. The sessions started with kit inspection followed by lessons on weaponry or map reading. An extremely strict code of discipline was enforced during these classes, especially when dismantling weapons and he would watch with an eagle eye, missing nothing. If any of us seemed to be struggling he would quickly spot that there was a problem and would immediately put it right. What he lacked in teaching skills he certainly made up for with his hands on approach. Several times a year we linked up with other units from around the country for manoeuvres or trips to the rifle range near to Oakham in Leicestershire. This trip was especially exciting merely for the fact that whilst there we were allowed to fire live ammunition, obviously under very strict supervision. Imagine the stories to be told to mates at school. I think I spent about two years in the cadets culminating in a two-week stay on the east coast.

This huge tented camp was at Cromer and was operated by the regular army. There was the canteen or NAAFI and a round the clock guard, patrolled the entrance to the camp. There were military vehicles everywhere creating an amazing atmosphere. The highlight of this trip was the night manoeuvres somewhere just outside Cromer. There were several companies of boy soldiers who had all been driven to different locations but each with the same mission, to capture the lighthouse! The next two or three hours would turn out to be some of the most exciting of my young life. At precisely 2300 hrs we started our offensive led by Captain English. The lighthouse was being defended by a small platoon of regulars who must have spent several days preparing for this night. Moving forward clutching our .202 rifles - loaded with blanks - we edged our way towards our goal. Flares tripped by the inexperienced and unsuspecting cadets, lit up the night sky like November 5th. During this assault we spent most of the time crawling on our bellies through the bracken and dunes raising ourselves up occasionally onto one knee to let off a few rounds in the general direction of the lighthouse.

tea from a jam jar — Alfie Watson

It was during one of these moments when I inadvertently shot Captain English's beret clean off his head. He had popped up in front of me at the precise moment I'd started to slip down a small slope and as I slipped, let off a shot. The end of my rifle must have been about two or three feet away from his head when I pulled the trigger. Luckily he was not injured. Even though we were firing blanks, they can still cause harm at such close range. Unfortunately he was not a very forgiving man and cancelled my pass for the duration of my stay. So while my mates were off into town at night, I was made to do guard duty instead. To make matters worse, our platoon had been captured shortly after and returned to the camp.

This hadn't been the first time I'd upset the captain. On another occasion we had been marched down to the beach one beautiful sunny day for a swim and in my eagerness to be first into the sea, I had stripped to my baggy woollen swimming trunks and was hurtling towards the water. With the wind whistling in my ears and the sound of about twenty other cadets pounding the pebbled beach behind me, I didn't hear him screaming for me to stop, and dived – complete with beret - straight into the cold and very salty North Sea.

Sleeping arrangements in camp were about six or eight to a tent sharing with other lads from other platoons. This was a great opportunity to get to know each other and to interact, because once we were out of the tents, we were back with our own company and they were our competition.

One incident I shall never forget involved a cadet - who was from a company from Sheffield - who tried to get to know me a little too well. I was woken in the early hours of the morning with an erection. Not unusual you may think, for a lad of fourteen years of age. But what was unusual was that it was this cadets hand that had been responsible for it! My reaction was instinctive; I hit him full in the face with a clenched fist, while at the same time asking him what the fucking hell he thought he was doing.

The noise soon attracted the attention of one of the N.C.O's, who took him away somewhere, probably for his own safety. I had to give a verbatim account of what had happened to Captain English, who incidentally relented shortly after this event and gave me back my pass, - every cloud has a silver lining - and the incident was never mentioned again. I couldn't help thinking that this lad must have done something similar before. The story circulating the camp was that his parents had been contacted and asked to collect him.

Apart from this incident everything was great and I was enjoying my life as a boy soldier. It seemed that a large part of each day was taken up by kit cleaning, especially the boots, which had to shine like glass in order to impress not just the Captain but also the judges who would be constantly scrutinising each company or unit. We all had a secret way to achieve the best shine; I seem to remember mine was potato peelings followed by spit and polish. Billy cans also had to be in pristine condition for inspection, as did belts and gaiters that had been lovingly treated with generous amounts of best quality dubbing. We also had to take turns helping out in the cook house, doing things like potato peeling or cleaning the ovens and washing out pots and pans, all very boring but necessary.

Some days a route march would be organised where we had the use of an army lorry and driver to ferry us to a distant location. Three or four Companies would march one behind the other, with intermittent lifts providing a brief respite every three or four mile. I can still remember the sense of pride I felt whilst sitting in the back of that truck, with my chest puffed out and my rifle by my side. People would always notice us, and kids waved as we went past. I remember thinking; this must be the sort of feeling soldier's get on returning from war.

The downside of life at the Cromer camp, was that on the two Sundays that we spent there, we had to go to church. Wearing our dress uniform we were marched to the church, a distance of about three miles or so, attend the service, and promptly be marched back again. I never met anyone who enjoyed this 'debacle' apart, that is from the priest who was obviously not used to such a large congregation, and milked it for all it was worth. If these trips were an attempt to try to convert us, then I am absolutely sure that it didn't work and probably served to do just the opposite. We just couldn't get away from there fast enough when the service had finished and get back to camp and into our civilian clothes. The rest of the day was ours, to do with whatever we liked and we'd invariably end up on the beach. I grew up very fast whilst in the cadets and I considered it a very good grounding for my adult working life and would certainly be a consideration for a career, which was now not too far off.

Seventeen

SAD DAY

Just as kids today have mountain bikes, ours were called track bikes. They had no brakes on the back wheel, only the front.

The reason for this was, a fixed wheel sprocket on the rear which meant that the pedals rotated at the same rate as the wheel. It was not possible to peddle backwards and there were no gears, the handlebars were called cow horns, for obvious reasons. They were great fun to ride, but could be dangerous to the uninitiated. Barry's sister, Linda, had borrowed his bike one-day, and had reached a notoriously steep hill, when her legs couldn't keep up with the speed of the pedals. Sadly she was thrown off onto the road, right into the path of an oncoming bus, and killed instantly. Linda was only thirteen years old when she died and Barry, it seemed, would never get over it. Shortly afterwards his parent's split up and the family moved away. I have not seen him since. I have to say I had shared my first brief sexual experience with Linda only a week or so earlier.

Eighteen

NEXT STEP IS WORK

I was now approaching fifteen and should be seriously thinking about my future; at least that's what everyone kept telling me. The army life was the only life for me, or so I thought. I had placed all my hopes on joining up, well why not do something I enjoy, rather than spend my life in a factory? On application I was to find out that dreams sometimes came true but also got broken. I was devastated to be told that I was too young to join the men's army and too old for the boys, and would have to wait a couple of years before even being considered. This was a massive disappointment to me, as I had, since joining the cadets, felt that the army would be able to offer me a way of life that I would never get in civvy Street. I hadn't given any thought to an alternative to the army, but my parents had. "Get yourself in the hosiery, that's where the money is." This was the usual response whenever the subject was mentioned.

I'd always felt that coming from a council estate, we shouldn't set our sights on anything too ambitious but the hosiery trade didn't tempt me at all. One or two of my friends who lived in private properties on the edge of the estate, would aspire to greater things. I know one person in particular who went into the hotel business and finished up as the managing director years later, for the Holiday Inn group. Such examples were very rare indeed and from my sort of background you would be more likely to end up on a building site as a labourer, or working for the council as a dustbin man, or of course working in a factory.

During the months leading up to leaving, we were taken on various factory tours. This was, I imagine, meant to whet our appetite. We were taken to a shoe factory one-week and an engineering factory the next, then perhaps to a hosiery or printing plant, none of which appealed to me for one reason or another. All they were showing us was the way certain products were manufactured, there was never any mention of how much the pay would be and as far as I know, nobody ever asked. It did seem to me that Secondary Modern schools would provide the factory fodder whilst the Grammar schools would provide the professional or the white and blue collar workers. All that seemed a long way off anyway, I wasn't leaving until Easter and it was still only November.

As I grew older I seemed to tempt fate a little bit more or maybe I was getting some attitude. Whatever it was, I don't know, but I was certainly taking more risks. In the past I wouldn't dare buy fags in the local shops for fear of being caught. But here I was in the off licence just around the corner, doing just that, totally unaware that my dad was standing behind me. He had often asked me if I smoked and I'd always say, 'no dad, I can't even stand the smell'. I knew he didn't believe me but until he'd actually caught me, there wasn't much he could do about it. I swore I was just fetching them for my mate's dad, but he wasn't about to swallow that line, he'd already made up his mind that I was guilty anyway and he was looking forward to dishing out some punishment. He marched me home, sat me down close to the fire grate and offered me a cigarette from the packet I'd just bought. Now this confused me totally. Does he want me to take one? Proving once and for all that I did smoke, Or perhaps he'd had a change of heart and wanted a father and Son chat over a fag, after all he'd smoked all his live, and so it was a bit rich for him to preach to me about the evils of smoking. If the latter is true, then there was an opportunity here for a bit of father and son bonding, if I missed this chance it would be lost forever. I took the cigarette and he offered me a light, he also made me smoke the other nineteen from the pack, one after the other, insisting that I inhaled on each drag I made. As I slowly sank into a state of extreme nausea, his distant voice echoed around my head, which felt like it was entombed in a tin bucket. 'There's a method in what I'm doing', 'this is for your own good'; and 'you'll thank me one day'. Bullshit! He was a sadistic bastard and was enjoying every second of my torture. I was sick for a couple of days after this and fags tasted revolting, but I had to persevere. If I'd stopped smoking now, he would have won!

The careers officers were back and it would soon be decision time. I still had no idea what I'd be doing, but I was still being ably advised by my mother that the only way was the hosiery way. Look at your aunt Pearl; she's doing all right for herself! Why don't you have a word with her about it? She'll put you right. It wasn't that long ago that we were all forbidden from talking to her for some reason, obviously things had been patched up now.

Sue had left school about two years before me and had also ended up in the hosiery. She had trained to be a machinist and was now bringing home a very decent wage. Egged on by mother and dad she also tried to persuade me to follow in her footsteps, even offering to get me a job at 'her place'. She was handing over her entire wage packet unopened and was handed back some spending money. I'd hear her complaining bitterly about it and arguing that her friends mother only took £3, leaving her some money to save or to buy some new clothes. This always met with the same response. "We've kept you for nothing all these years"! Well it will soon be my turn to contribute to the family coffers. That'll be interesting!

With my working life about to start in a few days, I still hadn't got a job. My parents were warning that if I didn't get one, I'd be out on the street. "We're not going to keep you for nothing any longer" The pressure was getting very intense, "go and see if Pearl can get you a job at her place" "Sue can get you one" Hosiery, Hosiery, Hosiery, They couldn't think of anything else, I'm even hearing it in my sleep.

Well, the day has finally arrived; I'm starting work. My letter says that I must report to the office and ask for a Mr Brown and he would take me into the factory and introduce me to everyone. I knew as soon as I got inside that it wasn't for me, the workers were friendly enough but it was the smell that I knew I couldn't stand. The shoe trade was not for me. I left after about a week or so, just as soon as I'd secured another job, in the hosiery!

    I started work at G.Stibbe & Co. Ltd, an extremely well established hosiery manufacturer here in Leicester. I was to be trained as a knitter. My first impression of the place was, 'what a shit hole', with boxes of assorted yarns in an array of colours occupying every available bit of floor space, and everywhere covered in a layer of fluff about 2 inch thick. How could people be expected to work in conditions like this? Apart from the knitting machines, which seemed to be scattered around randomly, there were oil drums, oil cans, rubbish boxes containing mouldy part eaten sandwiches and rotting fruit, and various machine parts, all appearing to have been left where they fell. Even the windows were covered in a layer of fluff, and looked like they'd never been cleaned, well certainly not on the inside anyway. Some were broken and had been stuffed with cotton fabric to keep out the draught. Empty upturned cardboard yarn boxes provided a table, where two or three workers were sitting eating their snack during the morning tea break. The table was adorned with part empty milk bottles, some containing sour milk and all kinds of other rubbish, what a disgusting sight! Mouse droppings, not surprisingly, were everywhere, as were the shallow boxes of poison bait. Drive shafts occupied the length of the room, hanging from the ceiling. These were connected to the machines below, via another shaft with leather belts with various sized pulleys, Kris crossing the room, and from a distance, looked like a giant leather web. The air was full of very fine particles of fluff or lint, which the occasional ray of sunshine from a broken pane, would highlight.

This was a very depressing sight and I'm wondering what the hell I've let myself in for. Apart from the whiff of sour milk and decaying food, the smell wasn't too bad, compared to the shoe factory anyway. I was introduced to Des. Who would be my foreman and my mentor during my training period. A slim handsome man around thirty years old, with already greying sideburns he looked very authoritarian in his brown smock with its breast pocket filled with pens and I liked him immediately. His first words to me were to warn me of the dangers when walking between the machines. With the drive belts crossing diagonally overhead it would be so easy to get my hair or any loose clothing caught up in them. Since I was already nearly six-foot tall and with a mop of very curly hair, I knew that I would have to be extra careful.

The knitter, who was to train me, was named Cyril. He was in his fifties, short and stocky, with bow legs, bold as a coot and a serious problem with body odour, and as if to add insult to injury, he took snuff as well (finely ground tobacco inhaled into his nose) which was evident by the brown stains on his clothes. Always wearing the same dark trousers, waistcoat and shirt, with sleeves rolled up, Cyril seemed locked into a time warp from a long ago Victorian period. Luckily there were other younger men working in the same room and I soon got to know them and I came to enjoy the friendly banter and the teasing that seemed to keep them going and obviously also helped them to get through the days. Playing tricks on

Cyril was by far their favourite pastime. Of course, I realised much of it was put on for my benefit though, and it did make me feel at ease. He was an extremely good sport though and took most of it in good fun, but there were times when they went more than a little bit too far. Either there was no water at home, or perhaps he didn't have the time, but every morning, before starting up his machines, always removing his waistcoat first he would wash himself at the small grubby sink which was situated outside the toilet. This I was to find out later was used by the mechanics to pour anything and everything, including dirty oil. No wonder it was so filthy and would always remain that way while I was employed there.

One day someone had decided to use this opportunity to mix pepper in with his snuff before placing it back into his waistcoat pocket. It must have looked, and smelt like the real thing to him, because, as we all stood slyly watching from a safe distance, he proceeded to push it habitually into one nostril and then the other without even flinching. The chaps were falling about laughing, the fact that he took it without knowing, was just as funny to them. I think I will like it here. There was nothing anyone could do now except to wait until he went for his constitutional in about an hour's time. Like clockwork Cyril always went at the same time each morning and as usual he would always remove his waistcoat, so this was their chance. Something else would be added; I think it was cigarette ash. He had barely been out of the toilet for five minutes, when all hell was let loose. Everybody was laughing loudly, as he pointed an accusing finger at each one of us.

tea from a jam jar   *Alfie Watson*

During fits of sneezing and coughing, it soon became clear that he thought this was the last straw and wasn't going to rest until whoever was responsible was brought to book. The factory manager got involved and issued a very stern warning, about such pranks and the obvious dangers of larking about in such a dangerous environment. He made it quite clear; as his eyes purposefully scanned each and every one of us, that if he should find out whoever was responsible, they would be sacked on the spot. Needless to say he was very unlikely to do that.

Because I had not shown much interest at school, I had been constantly reminded, that I'd have to 'pull my socks up' when I started work. Or told, 'you won't be able to mess around when you start there'. Well these lads never did much of anything else but mess around! It was one laugh after another, there really was, never a dull moment.

The word on the street whenever I would mention who I was working for was extremely positive. It seemed that Stibbe's was 'a good firm to work for', but I could never understand why people said this, unless they were confusing us with the engineering branch of the company, where young boys served three year apprenticeships after which time their wages would rise dramatically. Here the working conditions were so appalling and wages so low, it's a wonder anyone worked there at all. My starting pay was a measly £3-10s (£3-50p). Working hours were from eight am until six at night on weekdays, and eight am until twelve noon on Saturday's, making a 45-hour week. This was equal to about 6½p an hour.

As with Sue before me, all my wages had to be handed over to my mam on Friday and I would be given Ten Shilling's (fifty pence) back. Many of my mates were earning more than double this amount in the building trade or on the dustbins. I didn't mind that too much, I just loved going to work it was such a good crack. In any case, if I had earned more, my mother would only have taken more.

Nineteen

HUMILIATION

As long as I had my fags, I was all right, you had to smoke in those days, especially at work, it was considered to be antisocial if you didn't. Every half an hour we'd all cram ourselves into the toilet area and light up; there'd be maybe five or six of us standing in an area of about three foot by six. The one thing in the boss's favour was that we wouldn't be in there very long, for fear of choking to death. Being the youngest I was often the brunt of their jokes, and it was at one of these fag breaks that I was made too look a proper prat. The conversation was, as always, about sex, and this particular day it was about masturbation, with everyone's jokes and comments directed at me, being the new boy. Anxious to impress I would join in whenever I had the chance, always picking my words carefully, trying to fend off the jibes and always trying hard to avoid humiliation. Someone started to crack a joke relating to bath times, and had interrupted himself to asked, whilst looking around the group but mostly at me, if I knew what sperm looked like, floating in the bath. Without thinking I answered yes! oops!!

Lunch breaks were half an hour long, enough time to work up a sweat, and an appetite, playing football or cricket in the factory yard. There was always plenty of time to eat lunch when we were back in the factory, and on the boss's time.

This for now was quality time. It was the time to take some proper exercise and breathe in some fresh air, before returning to the hot, sweaty factory, where we would stay until six o'clock. And I can assure the reader that every man jack of us would be at the clocking machine at one minute to six and be gone by one minute past. We could not have vacated the premises any quicker if there'd been a fire. I for one couldn't wait to leap onto my bike and peddle for home, although I can't imagine why. I suppose it was about being free and escaping from the workhouse. Each day I used to race against the clock, weaving in and out of the traffic and whenever a clear stretch of road presented itself I'd put my head down and peddle like crazy in an attempt to beat my previous best time. I'd have my dinner, such as it was, and be out with my mates before seven o'clock. I couldn't stay in that house any longer than was absolutely necessary.

It had now been decreed by my dad that I would have to be in by ten thirty, 'now that I was working' and 10.30 pm meant 10.30 pm, one minute late and I would be in trouble as the door was locked, as if on a time switch. Even though I was now paying for my right to stay there, I was never given a key. All the kids were tucked up in bed well before eight o'clock and mam wouldn't be far behind them. Dad would wait until the older ones were safely indoors before retiring himself. Sue, who was two years older than me was made to be in at 9pm, and she argued constantly at the unfairness, especially the fact that I was younger and allowed an extra hour. The response was always the same, you're a girl. I was

tea from a jam jar — Alfie Watson

always the last to arrive and often late when he'd then make me wait outside, especially during the winter months until he felt like opening the door. Then I'd then be subjected to a verbal attack which would possibly last ten to fifteen minutes, when he'd launch into his favourite rhetoric, like, "your under my roof and you'll do as I tell you" and, if you don't like it "You know what you can do." My big mistake was to answer back, as this was like pouring petrol on an already blazing fire. As soon as we reached this stage, the next step would be physical violence which ended in someone getting hurt, and that "someone" was always me, I'd have the weal marks all over my arms as proof. Regardless of how much I detested him, and however much he made me suffer, it never occurred to me to retaliate. The problem was that he knew this and there were no limits to how far he would go to make his point.

Arriving home late on one particular night, I found the house in total darkness with all the doors locked and bolted. After realising that he wasn't going to answer my knocks I decided to try to break in. It was a severely cold night and dressed in just shirtsleeves, I started to prise open a small window leading to the kitchen that had been left unusually slightly open. After several abortive efforts, because my fingers were so cold, I finally managed to get it open. The cold was unbearable so I retreated to the outside toilet in an attempt to get some warmth from the small oil lamp - there to prevent the pipes from freezing - and also to get my breath back ready for the final assault. I'm not sure what time it was by this stage, but I imagine it must have been in the early hours of the morning. I was desperately cold now as I squeezed myself, head first through this tiny opening. Once I was far enough through I reached down to the sink and somehow managed to pull myself the rest of the way in without making too much noise. Shaking with fear, cold and exhaustion I climbed down to the floor and in the darkness put my foot directly into a bucket of shitty nappies that had been left there to soak overnight. At this precise moment the kitchen light came on. Startled and dazzled by the glare I found myself being bundled backwards towards the back door and out again. From behind the door, as the bolts were being slid across and the house made secure once more, he delivered his warnings and threats. He must have spent ages standing there in the darkness waiting for me to land in that strategically placed bucket.

I spent the next few hours shivering in the outside toilet, in wet and smelly socks, with just the lamp to keep me warm. I saw the kitchen light come on, this must be him getting washed and ready for work. He's bound to come for a piss, everyone I know needs a piss as soon as they wake up, so he'll be out soon and then perhaps he'll relent and let me in. Some time later I heard the front door close as he left for work. He must have pissed down the sink, sooner than confront me. Sue let me in minutes later, she empathised with me as she suffered from similar restraints on her life, but thankfully she had never been locked out. This was my dad's way of making his point, it did little to change me, quite the contrary, but it did make an impact otherwise I wouldn't be

tea from a jam jar — Alfie Watson

able to remember it so clearly today.

Summer holidays would be upon us soon, when, come the first two weeks in August, the whole country would be taking a rest from work. Those fortunate enough to be able to afford a holiday would join the millions of others heading for the coast. The first Friday and Saturday in August saw a mass exodus, with coaches and trains in great demand. Most folk on the estate were more or less in the same financial situation, so at best could only afford a day trip somewhere, usually Skegness or Chapel St Leonards. Those poor unfortunates such as us, stayed in what had become a ghost town. Those two weeks felt like an eternity. The seemingly endless days were occupied mainly with our latest pastime. Shooting birds, that's what we did, for no other reason than that they provided a target, with the local spinney providing us with plenty of prey. Not every one of us was lucky enough to possess a gun, so there was a lot of sharing going on. I had acquired an air pistol, but usually air rifles were used. Pete, my new mate and shooting partner shared mine. We spent the day shooting at mainly hedge sparrows and blue tits, having one shot each alternately, with the one who registered the most kills being the winner. The lads with the rifles usually came out on top because they were much easier to hold steady than a pistol. It was vital that my parents didn't find out that I had a gun, so Pete kept it at his house. They had high morals when it came to the harming of birds, although neither one was loathe to inflicting violence on me at every possible opportunity.

One morning during that summer holiday fortnight, I was

tea from a jam jar   *Alfie Watson*

hanging about waiting for Pete when Sue came from the house with a large bag of goodies that she had prepared for a day out with a couple of her mates, and she was just waiting for them to arrive. One of these friends was absolutely drop dead gorgeous and I was just showing off by larking about with their picnic bag. I was holding it up above my head, and was pretending to run off with it when I tripped, smashing it to the ground, breaking the two bottles that were in there. This soaked the entire contents of the bag of sandwiches and biscuits with dandelion and burdock pop. Naturally, Sue was not best pleased and started screaming abuse at me, bringing it to the attention of dad, who had been busying himself in the back garden. The full force of his hand came down across my head and I knew I was in for one hell of a beating. He dragged me inside the house, and thrashed me mercilessly with his favourite leather belt; only stopping when he realised I was bleeding. I had cut my hand when I was trying desperately to salvage some of the bags contents. He didn't know that, and I wasn't about to tell him. He'd finished with me now and I was sent to my bedroom for the rest of the day, to nurse my wounds, which would likely take several days to disappear. Far worse than the beating, was the fact that the girl I was attempting to impress had witnessed it all and I doubt she was impressed either. By the time I'd reached my bedroom, I could hear him through the open window, making polite conversation with our next-door neighbour over the garden fence as if nothing had happened.

    Who would believe that just a few minutes ago, he had

thoroughly beaten one of his own flesh and blood and all this because of a couple of broken bottles of pop. What would he do to me if he ever found out about the air pistol? This was to be the format for the entire fortnight, with my dad watching my every move, and wanting to know where I'd been and who with. He invariably didn't approve of whoever I was with or where I'd been. So I had to lie constantly

I'm longing to get back to work. Des has promised to increase my wages considerably when I go back, so who knows, I may be able to afford to leave home soon.

Back at work after the holiday, life started to resemble normality again. I'd missed all the lad's and was glad to be back amongst friends. The first few hours of the day were taken up with discussions about everyone's holidays, interspersed with a few pranks. A new boy had started and was being shown around. The scene was reminiscent of the day four months earlier, when I had just started, with Cyril being the butt of all the jokes again. This time someone had squirted oil onto one of his drive belts causing it to slip, and of course he was rising to the bait as usual. The larking about continued all day, with the new boy put suitably at ease. Des was true to his word and I was now asked to run three machines, almost a full set, with the guarantee that my pay would increase accordingly. What a difference two weeks could make. Before the holiday I was the tea boy, and general lackey but now, here I was almost a fully trained knitter, with a boy making my tea.

tea from a jam jar — Alfie Watson

Arriving home with my first big weeks wage of around £12, I handed it over unopened as I always did. My mother, weeks away from another birth, took the ten pounds and handed me two. This didn't go down too well with me, and another argument soon started when the same old lines popped up again, "we've fed and clothed you all these years and this is the thanks we get" Blah! Blah! Blah! Most of my mates who were at work, were paying, what was known as board. This was usually set at around three pounds a week. I was determined that that's what I wanted to do, but mother had her own ideas about that, she wanted more. I suppose with having another mouth to feed shortly it was to be expected. But the fact that there would soon be eight kids to provide for was not my fault or my problem.

After several weeks and much discussion, or I should say arguing, I reluctantly agreed that I would pay five pounds a week. My take home pay had been fairly consistent for a few weeks now, but I knew that I still hadn't reached my full earnings potential. When, in time, I was capable of managing the fourth machine; my wages should be increased by about 25%, meaning I should be taking home about £16. I was so well off now, even my mates, who had been bragging a couple of months earlier were amazed, but it wasn't going to last. After talking to my mates and comparing deductions, it became obvious that I wasn't paying anywhere near enough tax. A check with the wages office at work and they revealed that my tax code was wrong and that when it had been corrected, I should expect to be paying quite a bit more in income tax. I think my mother had spotted this when she agreed to let me pay board. She must have compared my wage slip with my dad's.

After a few weeks, the outstanding tax had been paid back, and I was running the fourth machine, I was again taking home about twelve pounds. Well it still left me with about seven to spend on myself, so I was well pleased, but it still hurt to think that I was paying almost double the amount of board that any of my mates were paying. It wasn't long after, that Sue decided she also wanted to pay board, which was fixed at three pounds! Over the ensuing weeks I discovered that I was also expected to occasionally pay for the Sunday meat joint and also put money in the meter from my own pocket whenever I had a bath.

Ever since junior school, I had dreamt of leaving home and that day would not be too far off. The sleeping arrangements were being changed again to make way for another home birth. This time it was another brother to be named Paul and bringing the family total to 10. Where the hell are we all going to sleep?

Twenty

A LESSON ABOUT LIFE

One beautiful summer day, I was enjoying a chat during my lunch break, with a few girls from the office. We were sitting on the loading bay, which faced out directly on to the street, when we found ourselves being eyed up by three youths and two teenage girls who were quite obviously intent on causing some trouble. As they got closer, I recognised one of the boys as an old school friend and I thought he'd recognised me as they crossed the street and headed menacingly towards us. In order to try to defuse what looked like becoming a very tense situation, I shouted hello to him, using his first name. This seemed, for some reason, to antagonise the other gang members, who then demanded to know, 'who the fuck I was talking to.' It was clear that I was their target, but I had no idea why, other than wanting to impress the girls they were with or maybe the ones I was with. It was at that point that we quickly fled inside the factory shutting the large wooden sliding doors behind us. All that afternoon, their parting words would haunt me, 'we'll see you later Watson' and I knew they meant it.

That afternoon I started to prepare for the inevitable. I spent every spare moment making myself a knuckle-duster, thinking that it might help to even things up a bit. I think I also felt safe in the knowledge that, should the worst happen,

tea from a jam jar   *Alfie Watson*

there'd be enough of my work mates around to help me out. How naïve I was then and some say I still am.

    This day I learned a very valuable lesson and that was, that in times of need you're on your own. They were there all right, waiting opposite the car park gates. Four of them were sitting at the kerbside. As I walked towards them I was surrounded by fellow workers and was feeling quite secure. They didn't make a move. I collected my bike from the rack and headed back toward them. It was the only exit. So armed with my knuckle-duster I prepared to meet my fate. Cometh the hour! Cometh the man! As the saying goes. As I rode past them they dragged me from my bike and dished out one hell of a beating; I didn't stand a chance. As I lay on the floor, with the kicks reigning in, I could see and hear vehicles leaving the car park, some barely half a metre from my head but they all drove past. They left me lying in the road with my bike on top of me. Badly cut and bruised, I made my way home, thankful that I'd still got all my teeth. There would be no racing against the clock tonight. My bike had also taken a bashing, with both wheels having been buckled during the mêlée. I managed to straighten the wheels out by standing on them so I could push it home, although I don't know why I didn't just dump it. I think it was during my long walk home that I decided I would buy myself a new one; after all I was earning enough money now.

    It was late when I arrived home and my dinner, which was being kept warm on top of a saucepan of boiling water, was totally inedible. I still had to explain to my mother, who hated to see a meal ruined, why I was late. All questions about my injuries were met with the same reply. I fell off my bike! Knowing that my future at Stibbe's was fairly secure, and that my wages could only get better, I ordered a bike from next doors Kays catalogue. I think it cost around £20 with the repayments of Ten Shillings (50p) a week, spread over forty weeks.

My green and yellow racing bike duly arrived, complete with racing handlebars; dynamo powered lights and multiple gears. Riding this around Braunstone would turn a few heads, it was flash!!! and I travelled miles on that bike, it became my pride and joy. Shooting birds now no longer interested to me - to be absolutely honest it never really did - mainly because I was such a lousy shot anyway. Pete bought my gun and my old bike from me and he was welcome to them.

Weekends were now an absolute joy, especially during the summer months. I would pack the rear panniers with crisps, biscuits and pop etc. and be off, anywhere, it didn't matter where, just as long as I was on the road. Bradgate Park, home of Lady Jane Grey, queen of sixteenth century England, was a regular haunt of mine as was Nottingham castle. Distance was never a problem. I had another new friend now who had also just bought a new bike, Tom was his name, but he insisted on being called Tommy. He enjoyed biking as much as I did, so we hit it off just great. Tommy had also recently left school but hadn't yet started work. He was very much like me in build, stature and age but was streets ahead when it came to looks. There were plenty of places to visit, but many could only be accessed by road, (no cycle lanes in those days) and they could prove to be very dangerous indeed, especially the ones out in the countryside with narrow lanes and sharp bends. We had to take evasive action many times, narrowly avoiding on coming traffic which on one occasion was to leave Tommy lying upside down in a ditch, still with his fag in his mouth. It may have been this experience that prompted us to try a ride along the canal tow-paths wherever possible; at least there would be no speeding cars to lookout for.

These canal tow paths were a new adventure for us. Some stretches were quite wide and the gravel path provided a good surface for cycling. But other parts were a formidable challenge made worse by the many fishermen who lined the banks, their spare rods, baskets and bikes strewn beside them. Nevertheless we found that we loved it. The paths were often uneven and extremely narrow but had to be negotiated from the saddle, no matter how slow we rode. To dismount always meant failure. The only time this was allowed was if we had to mend one of the many punctures we managed to get whilst riding along there, or when we had to negotiate a narrow canal bridge. This meant carrying the bikes up the many steps on one side of the bridge and down the others on the other, but at least this gave us a chance to have a fag! Wildlife was in abundance along the canal, with the quieter stretches having a large population of water rats or perhaps otters or voles, I doubt we'd have known the difference. At the sound of our approaching bikes they plopped into the water from their bank side holes a few yards ahead, and swam to the opposite side to safety. There were times when I'd wish I still had my air pistol. On a good day out we could find ourselves in a Nottingham marina or even the castle, riding along the canal side all the way, whenever the track allowed. Because of the distance we travelled, it was often twilight before we'd start our journey home; the fading light made the adventure all the more exciting. It was strange the way we seemed to be riding that much faster the darker it got, and the tow-path was shown to be more uneven, exaggerated of course by the bouncing beam from our bike lamps. After a few long exciting and exhausting canal ride it became obvious to us that we were ruining the bikes. The wheels were too narrow for this type of track. My old bike would have faired better. It was a case of horses for courses.

It may have been because the darker nights were approaching, or because it was getting colder, but our keenness for cycling gradually waned. I still kept my bike in good condition though, using it to get to work and back and to run the odd errand. During one of our earlier cycling trips Tommy and I had met a lad of our own age whose dad owned an ice cream company. Johnny Massarella was his name and he tried very hard to get us to join him in, what to us seemed like an extremely original idea, purely on a part time basis. The proposition was that he had been given two horses and two carts and he wanted us to take them onto the estate and sell ice cream from them. His dad- a very well known local business man - clearly wanted to see whether he could make it work and Johnny was determined to do just that. Curious to find out more, we decided that we'd pay him a visit and found him busy painting one of the ice cream carts in his fathers company colours. He was anxious to get his carts up and running by May next year. If we decided to do it, it would mean that we'd have to be at the yard by about 7am, collect the horses from the field feed and harness them and load up the cart. Payment would be purely on a commission basis, so if we didn't sell we didn't earn. We agreed to give it a try, even though what either of us knew about horses could have been written in capital letters on the back of a postage stamp. It sounded like it might be good fun so we promised to see him again in April the next year.

Christmas was fast approaching, and it was time to start thinking about presents. Because I was now at work and earning a reasonable wage I was expected to buy for the whole family. This worked out rather expensive, especially since I was also asked to contribute to the food costs. It was my own fault; I shouldn't have let them know what I was earning. I only did it to show my dad that I could earn more than him. The kids would usually get a tin of Bluebird toffee's each or a small game of some description. It was with reluctance that I bought my parents anything at all, especially my dad. I thought I'd buy him some fags and my mam some smellies. Anyway with only weeks to go I still hadn't bought any adult presents and I was a bit short of cash as I'd been spending rather a lot on myself lately. I'd just bought my first suit along with all the accessories from "Jackson's The Tailors", where the smart set shopped back then in Leicester. I had never had any trouble getting into the local pub, The Shakespeare, but dressed in this gear I could get in anywhere and did, consequently spending loads more of my pay on booze.

Because myself and a few mates had just knocked off the local chemist, the theme for presents this year would be toiletries and cosmetics. All the booty had to be hidden away for a few days until the "heat was off", as they say in the underworld! People who were not normally considered for a gift were now on my list; well we had to get rid of it all as quick as possible. All three of my uncles received shaving kits and my two aunts got perfume. It was certainly a good way to make friends and I was suddenly very very popular. Even the caretaker at my old school got an old spice gift set in appreciation for selling me the odd fag when I was desperate. My barber got some under arm deodorant, which he was desperately in need of but I always reckoned he'd given it to someone else as a present, because he never smelt any better. I kept a supply of breath fresheners back for myself, so my dad wouldn't smell the booze on me. I wonder what he would have done, had he caught me. Perhaps I'd have been sat down in front of the fire and forced to drink pint after pint of Red Barrel, the popular drink at the time.

One very strange thing happened shortly after this period of distributing the loot. One morning a whisper through my bedroom door from one of my sisters, who slept in the front bedroom, announced that there was a copper outside our house. Well, I very nearly shit myself as I ran to a front

tea from a jam jar   *Alfie Watson*

window only to confirm what she had said. Oh my god, what shall I do? Have they got all the other gang members in custody? Has somebody blown the whistle on us? How much do they know? It wasn't like in today's world, a call on the mobile to a mate would be all it would take. We had no phones at all and I had no way of making contact with anybody. The things that went through my head during this period of not knowing was incredible. For instance, what prison would I go to? How many years will I get? Was I really the leader? If so, will I get a longer sentence? I was now starting to feel extremely sick and must have looked terrible. My dad was just leaving for work and I heard him say to my mam how stupid he thought the police were to be standing there. By now I had plucked up enough courage to creep halfway down the stairs in order to hear what was being said. I heard Sue ask my mam what he was doing there and she replied that they were there because someone had been stealing the milk from our doorstep on a couple of mornings earlier and your dad had reported it. Jesus Christ, what a relief! I felt like I'd escaped the gallows. In those last few minutes I had been to hell and back. How ridiculous could they get. Waiting almost on the doorstep, Well they certainly wouldn't get the thief now, especially as I wasn't likely to pinch another while he stood there.

   Christmas came and went, and I for one was glad. It was sheer hell in our house, with the kids arguing and fighting over toys and dad getting under mam's feet so they were constantly bickering as well. I had made sure that I was out of the house for most of the day, returning only at meal times or to change my clothes. We'd enjoyed some really good nights out at the Westend working men's club, where we would usually get in without question. It was basically dependent on who was on the door at the time. But even if there was a problem over our ages or our membership details, we'd always manage to get in somehow; maybe as a guest of someone we knew, or, sometimes we would wait outside and sneak in while the doorman was distracted. Either way we never caused any bother and we got on well with the regulars. I often wondered why we were refused entry at some pubs and clubs. We were always well dressed and both stood around six feet tall. Maybe it was because we were so well dressed that we drew attention to ourselves, or perhaps it was our spotty boyish faces that gave us away.

tea from a jam jar *Alfie Watson*

Twenty-one

SPECIAL BIRTHDAY

With Christmas over it was back to work again, and with everyone short of cash, overtime was sought by many of us. I managed to get some, emptying the fluff bins. These were t large silos' that collected all the fluff that was created during the brushing process to produce sweatshirt fabric. They were Two of them, big enough to hold a week's supply of fluff but it was vitally important that they were emptied every week, to avoid the risk of fire. This was only possible on each Saturday afternoon after work ceased for the week. It didn't take me long to realise why I got the job. No one else wanted it! On opening the door to the first silo I was confronted with a solid wall of very tightly compacted fluff about ten foot high, in an assortment of colours which reminded me of a jar of multi coloured khali that I used to buy from our local sweet shop. My job was to empty this fluff into large canvass bags, a handful at a time. I was provided with a boiler suit, a hat and a mask, and left to get on with it. If I was expected to empty both bins in four hours, which were the usual overtime hours for a Saturday, then someone had grossly under estimated the size of the task or my will to perform it.

After a couple of hours without a break I'd hardly made any impression and had filled about ten bags, climbing a hill of sand comes to mind. The temperature inside these things was unbelievably hot, so it wasn't possible to stay in there for more than five minutes at a time. I think I managed to empty about three-quarters of the contents of one silo, filling about twenty bags. I had no one to report to, as there was no supervisor to watch over me on Saturday's, so after doing as much as I could do or wanted to do, I headed off home.

It was around the middle of the next week when the fire alarms started to wail and the entire factory was evacuated. Like everyone else, I thought it was a false alarm or a system check as it usually was. Either way it was an opportunity to gather in the car park and have a fag. Word soon got around that it was the fluff bins and it had been the other bin- the one I hadn't even opened - that had started to smoulder, bringing the brushing plant to a stand still. The fire brigade arrived to damp down and insisted that all the fluff be removed before they would allow the plant to restart. The brushing machine operators emptied both in record time, perhaps because it was a lot easier to remove whilst wet, and production was soon restarted. I was given the biggest bollocking of my working life to date, but from then on, it was declared the bin emptying would require two men from now on. So it was good to see that some good came out of it all. The new boy in the knitting room, Terry or Tes, as he liked to be called, joined me in the bins for the next few weeks. It was still a thankless job but it was much easier and more fun with some friendly company to help me. I decided to stick it out until April, when I would start working for Johnny Masserella, selling his ice cream.

tea from a jam jar   *Alfie Watson*

Little did I know, when I awoke on this wet and windy day in March, what drama was going to unfold. I was not at work for some reason; I think it must have been a holiday, because I would never miss work in order stay at home voluntarily. Mam asked me to go to the shops, or rather she ordered me to go. I knew this meant that she wanted something on tick or book, (credit) most people on the estate wouldn't have survived without this service. My mother rarely went to the shops and why would she, with an army of kids to call on, but she would definitely never belittle herself when tick was required. So off I went, but rather than take my bike, because it had a puncture, I decided to use my mother's rickety old boneshaker, well! It was only a few hundred yards to Miss Shipman's. Having already had a history of forgetting things whenever I was sent on errands. I always had to empty my mind of everything else, just to remember what I was going for. This, I'm sure is the reason I came home without the bike, as had once happened in the past, when I had come back without baby Stephen and his pram, my newest brother at the time, Luckily for me then, I had remembered before getting all the way back home, so no one got to know about it and there was no damage done. This time I had reached the front door before I'd realised what I had done and raced back to the shop as fast as my legs could possibly carry me, only to find that it had gone. My mother went totally ballistic and as usual she couldn't wait for my dad to come through the door before she started screaming to him about what I'd done.

Our Alfie's gone and got my bike nicked. I swear he's done

it on purpose, probably sold it to one of his mates for beer money. You're gonna have to teach him a lesson; he never wanted to go in the first place. Thinks he's above going on errands now he's at work, he's done this out of spite, believe me Alf. What's he doing with you're bike anyway? He'd said, what's wrong with his? He's just too idle to pump the tyres up I suppose. With all these muddled accusations, lies and questions, ringing in my head, I could sense I was about to get another beating and she wasn't going to give up yelling until I did. I had moved into the kitchen now and shut the door, sitting there waiting for the inevitable, as I had done on many occasions before, watching the door handle, knowing that as soon as it began to turn, my punishment wouldn't be far behind. The door flew open and smashed against the wall behind it, as he stormed towards me. I was shaking with fear of what was about to come, as with previous beatings, it never ever entered my head to fight back. He strode right passed me, not saying a word, his eye's almost popping from their sockets. I've seen him like this before and I knew I wasn't going to get of the hook that easily. I thought, It was his way of making me stew, and I knew that worst was to come. He marched straight into his shed and the house fell silent. This silence was broken a few minutes later by the sound of metal smashing onto metal. As I watched from the kitchen window, I witnessed the total destruction of my bike; I was struggling to stop myself from crying. He was literally using an axe to reduce my beautiful green and yellow bike to scrap. I knew from the mood he was in that worse was to come my way. I also knew from previous hidings that the stronger he responded to my mam's demands, the happier their relationship became, for a while.

I decided that I would take my chance to get the hell out of there before he came back into the house; I made my escape through the front door and into the street, grabbing my overcoat off the banister on the way. My ability to run fast came in useful and within minutes I was on the park. I found a good vantage point so I could see the comings and goings. I would have enough time to hide should he come looking for me, though I doubted he would. As darkness began to fall, it was obvious that he wouldn't be coming now. I made my way to "Roland's", the estates fish and chip shop, where I filled myself with chips and scratchings, and headed for the Shakespeare. I met up with Joe, an old school pal and a few beers later we were heading home. Well he was, but I don't know where the hell I will lay my head tonight. I hadn't told any body about the days events. In a way I sort of felt embarrassed that I had a dad who was capable of doing such a thing. I spent that night sleeping on a bench in the parks pavilion; the date was 25th March 1961, my 16th birthday. And it was bitterly cold.

The following day I bumped into Mark, one of our "gang" who told his mam of my plight, and she kindly took me in. It was Saturday and Mark introduced me to lunch time drinking in the local working men's club. I was totally unaware of the effects of daytime drinking and soon started to feel quit pissed but I put it down to the fact that I had not slept well on the park. Anyway I think Mark realised I needed a kip badly so we headed back to his house a little earlier than he would normally have done. This house was beautiful, with carpets wall to wall instead of lino, which is all I'd ever seen. It was exceptionally homely and I was soon made to feel very much at ease. Soon we were sitting down to pie and chips, that's a whole pie each, which was a real treat for me, usually a pie would be split four ways at our house, and her home made chips were something else too. She seemed to be what every mother should be, kind, loving and caring. Dinner finished, I asked if she would mind if I took a kip. She was absolutely fine and showed me to Dales room where I flaked out for a couple of hours waking feeling completely refreshed. This is the first time I had witnessed how another family outside of my relatives, lived and it was not what I was used to at all. Admittedly Mark was an only child, so that made a massive difference. His mother worshipped the ground he walked on, that was plain for all to see. I was immediately accepted by her and treated in exactly the same way. I must admit to feeling rather uncomfortable and embarrassed at all the kindness they were showing towards me and each other.

His dad was a military man, very upright and well spoken, but only when he was spoken to. He used the same drinking club as Mark and they often went out together. They had a lovely relationship, more like mates, than father and Son. During the writing of this diary, and after the death of both of his parents, Mark discovered that his real dad had originated from Canada and was also now deceased. He had been a serving soldier in England during the war, stationed on

tea from a jam jar   Alfie Watson

Braunstone Park, when he met and had a fling with his mother. She was a lovely kind lady who I would have loved to have had as a mother. She was extremely pretty and in her mid thirties with a beautiful friendly smile, it's little wonder that she had attracted the yanks all those years ago. I was absolutely amazed that Mark was never told of this, he certainly would never have guessed from the way he was treated by his dad (step dad.)

Mark's home was a few streets away from my house and I badly needed to get some clothes. I knew that my mother wouldn't be in the house because she had recently started work at the Co-op restaurant in town and never got in till about 6.30pm on Saturdays. I expected my dad would be there though, but hopefully he'd be either in his shed or in the back garden where he seemed to spend most of his time. I suspect to keep out of mothers way. He may even be asleep, which is something else he did a lot of, especially when mam was at work. Anyway whatever happened I had to have a change of clothes for tonight and for work on Monday. Luckily for me my big sister Sue opened the door explaining that I'd better be quick because he'd only gone round the bookies to collect some winnings from the days racing. This was another one of his pleasures along with smoking and beating me. The bookies were illegal and operated from a council house opposite my grandparents house, about two or three minutes walk away. Luckily enough, there was time for me to tell Sue where I was staying and grab my cherished shadow check, Italian style suit, with my winkle picker boots and my bootlace tie. I chucked my work clothes in a dirty pillow case and legged it out of there, so relieved not to have bumped into him.

Back at Marks home both he and his dad were waiting for me, all dressed up in their suits. Everyone made an effort and got dressed up to go out in those days and I was no exception. In my rush though, I had forgot to grab a shirt so Mark's dad lent me one of his. One of Mark's would have been more stylish but would have been far too big. Any way it nearly fitted me and I was grateful, beggars can't be choosers, as the saying goes. I loved the Braunstone and District club and that's where we headed on my Birthday weekend. I knew some of my uncles drank in there occasionally on Sunday lunchtime but what a surprise to see them there that night, just like a surprise party. My uncle Alan was there with his best mate and next-door neighbour, Mick. My Uncle Ted, auntie Pearl's husband, was also there so we joined them. What a great night we all had and they found out from Mark that it was my Birthday so wouldn't let me or Mark buy a round all night. Only problem was that they would not let me drink at my own pace either and soon the pints were lining up.

I walked or I should say, staggered the three or so miles back to Mark's home and by the time we arrived, my head had cleared quite a lot and all I could think off was bed. His mam opened the door to us; she must have been peeping through the curtains, waiting. You would have thought we had been away on a polar expedition or something for several months, by the way she welcomed us home. On walking into the living room, there on the table was a supper fit for a King. There were pork pies, a bone of ham and pickles and lots more stuff that I didn't even know the names of. There was enough food to feed all ten of my family for Sunday lunch. Boy did I tuck in, everything looked so tempting. I can remember his mam carving ham from the bone and making me a lovely doorstep of a sandwich of ham and beetroot, beautiful!

Soon it was off to my bed but I presumed it would be in a bed on my own. Not at all, I was in with Mark. I'm used to sleeping three in a bed, even having the younger brothers peeing up my back in their sleep, but this felt different, strange even, and certainly a first for me. As it happened, it turned out OK; after all it was a double bed. The room must have been recently decorated because the smell of paint was overwhelming. I managed to stay awake long enough to witness through partly closed eyes, Mark's mam come into the room, plant a kiss on his cheek, tuck him in and wind up his Mickey mouse clock. For heavens sake, he was nearly eighteen years old!!

I don't know why but some time later I awoke to the all too familiar rotating ceiling syndrome and an overwhelming urge to puke. I staggered blindly into one wall after another in a futile search for the door - although had I found it I would still have had to find the toilet - leaving a trail of ham and beetroot vomit in my wake. Finally, I found the window and flung it open emptying the entire contents of my gut on the path below. I can honestly say that I had never felt this ill before. But I'd never had so much to drink before either and I'd certainly never had a banquet at bedtime. On waking the next morning, I really didn't want to open my eyes; I barely dare look at the mess I had made.

Gradually as the dawn began to break I knew that the morning sunlight would soon begin baking the puke onto the walls, inside and out. As Mark lay snoring at my side, the realisation of what I had done slowly began to dawn on me. As I lay there surveying the nights work from the warmth of a lovely thick duvet (something else I'd never heard of before) I was totally overcome with guilt. I had vomited over two newly decorated walls, this much I could see from the bed, but what about outside? What mess had I made out there? Staggering from the bed I soon realised that the carpet had not escaped either and was also covered in this stinking foul mess. I opened the window and realised this night had really been a "nightmare".

The newly painted pebble dashed wall, although affected, didn't look too bad. What an embarrassment. How was I going to face Mark's parents after this? What a way to show my gratitude after they had made me feel so welcome. I was so wracked with guilt that I didn't think I would be able to face them again. Mark was not best pleased either when he finally woke to see and smell the state his room was in. Amazingly, yet again his mother was incredibly kind to me over it; saying, not to worry it will all wash off. Maybe she'd had to deal with a similar experience with Mark in the past. Whatever, she was so remarkably chilled. Even after all of

tea from a jam jar   *Alfie Watson*

this, I sat down with them to a cooked breakfast and it wasn't mentioned at all. After breakfast I cleaned the bedroom walls and the skirting boards which, amazingly cleaned up quite well. Meanwhile Mark and his dad were standing on the outside toilet roof, in the freezing cold March wind, his dad hosing the wall and Mark helping by sweeping it clean. My last night's supper disappeared down the drain leaving the wall perfectly clean. The only thing to do now was to clean the carpet, and get rid of the smell but Dales mam insisted that she would do this while we were out. Out! Out where? oh no! not there again, I thought!

Before I knew it, it was eleven o'clock and drinking time again. Mark and his dad were always at the door for opening time every Sunday lunch time, it was a religion. Making my excuses I headed off in the opposite direction, towards my house. When it came to drinking, I was out of my league there, and incidentally still am to this day. I really couldn't get away from there quick enough and knew I would need to find somewhere else to stay.

It was perfectly clear as I approached the front gate that news of my arrival had travelled via the good old jungle telegraph. Or perhaps it was just pure coincidence that my dad was waiting at the gate. I really had to swallow hard when I asked, in a sort of pleading voice, if I could come back. The answer was a resounding, NO!! As my heart sank and my eyes began to fill up, I spun away quickly and made my way to my Grandma's house. As I reached the gate, my Uncle Alan and his mate Mick were just leaving for the club,

tea from a jam jar   *Alfie Watson*

so I decided to tag along. The twenty or so minutes it took us to get there; I told what had happened. I'll speak to my mam he said, I'm sure she'll put you up. But the question I was asking myself now was, should I really be putting Gran in the firing line. After all, she'd done nothing wrong! We arrived at the club, but I only had a couple of pints, after last night's humiliation, perhaps I should stop drinking altogether. Mark and his dad were there, with Mark knocking them back as if his life depended on it. Anyway when they'd had their fill and we headed off back to Mark's, he gruffly told me I would be welcome to stay for dinner, an offer I was not about to refuse as I was absolutely starving. I could tell in his voice that his mum may say that I was welcome to stay but he certainly wasn't and I didn't blame him.

Arriving back I started to apologise again, forget it, no damage done, was the response. I was sincerely sorry and very embarrassed and she knew it. The smell of roast beef wafting through from the kitchen was more than enough to hide the smell of bleach which we had left behind earlier. A proper Sunday dinner duly arrived and every last bit was graciously if not leisurely devoured. It was really nice at Mark's, even after the antics of the previous night; I still felt really at home and relaxed in their company. Dinner out of the way and out came the board games with some television in between. Is this what home life was like everywhere? I wondered, cos it was certainly never like this at our house, I could never imagine my mam or dad playing any sort of game with us. As grateful and as comfortable as I was, I couldn't stay here for long. It was back to work tomorrow so I could ask around then. I would spend another night with Mark, but this time there would be no booze.

Twenty-two

MY LOVELY GRAN

When Mark and his dad invited me to go out to the Shakespeare with them that night, I declined and used the opportunity to visit my grandma, who seemed really pleased to see me. The door flung open and there she stood, all five feet of her, with arms outstretched, beckoning me across the threshold. I loved my Gran and it seemed she felt the same even if it was tinged with a degree of pity. She was a lovely lady with a big toothless smile. Her fingers on both hands were very misshaped because of arthritis, which must have been extremely painful. We had tea and biscuits as we talked about my predicament and what my dad, her son, had done, she was very upset about the way he'd behaved but immediately blamed my mother. As far as I was concerned it didn't matter particularly, who was to blame, I was out on a limb. She began to apologies that she could not put me up because there was no room. Interrupting, I said that's why I came round to see you, you don't have to be sorry, I've found somewhere to stay, and I'm fine. I could not have burdened her with my problems and the repercussions that would surely follow. There was another reason why I was not keen on stopping there and that was because the house was very dirty, filthy in fact, and personal hygiene wasn't that high on her list either. The underneath of her fingernails were black, her clothes were covered in dog hairs as was the settee, chairs and the large peg rug, lying in front of the hearth that the dog obviously thought was his bed. The kitchen in particular, as in my house, was where the men had their wash and shave. Still using the same towel that was used to dry the dishes. She would also easily have taken the prize for the worst cook- apart from her bread and butter pudding that is - on the estate without really trying very hard.

Around this time, frozen food was becoming popular and families everywhere were getting used to having a chicken for Sunday lunch, a nice change from shoulder of lamb. In those days, when a chicken was prepared for freezing at the poulterers, all its giblets were put into a plastic bag and stuffed back inside the carcass. On Thawing they were supposed to be removed, and could be used to make gravy. According to Uncle Alan , she had cooked the first one, still frozen with the bag still inside. He'd often tell that story to anyone who'd listen.

I learned first hand that she could not understand the concept of frozen food, when she arrived back from the shop one day with a frozen sponge cake and commented on how hard they were to slice compared to the old sort. I often wondered how such a lovely naive old lady could have produced a son like my dad. No, I have to admit, it would not have been pleasant staying there, but sometimes it was not possible to be choosy. This time I was all right for the time being but who knows what could be around the next corner.

tea from a jam jar *Alfie Watson*

Having made my way back to Mark's I was shocked to find that my dirty clothes had been washed and pressed. Now I really did feel bad about what I'd done. Anyway it was work tomorrow and I would hope someone would come up with a solution to my current homeless problem, and find me somewhere to stay. Mark and I went to bed at the same time but he was up at about 5am for his shift. He worked for a large hosiery manufacturer in the city, on a three rotating shift system. I, on the other hand didn't start till 8 am so I could have another couple of hours in bed. I was lying there thinking about getting up and what the day might hold for me when his mam brought me a cuppa. Thanking her for the tea, I promised that I would find somewhere else to stay, when I got to work. She made it perfectly clear that I didn't have to go, and then asked would I like a cooked breakfast to start the day, I declined because I wasn't sure what my stomach would make of it. It must have wondered where all of this weird and wonderful food had come from all of a sudden.

As soon as I arrived at work I headed for the toilets, and as usual everyone was there having the first communal fag of the day. Boy we must have stunk to high heaven to anyone who didn't smoke, these group fag fests would continue throughout the day, including tea and dinner breaks. I took my opportunity to mention my predicament when the bog was full. Straight away Des - the comedian amongst us - reckoned his mate, who had just recently lost his job, had a spare room, this gave me hope. Des Green was a great bloke, well they all were, but I really liked Des, he was a knitter, one of about ten, their ages ranging from sixteen to sixty. We were like a big family who would all look after each other in most things, but not when getting ones head kicked in, as I remember all too well. Everybody to a man in there said they would ask around for me, so I was feeling pretty sure I'd find somewhere.

Des took me back to his house that night, for dinner and then on to see his mate, Geoff, who was about the same age as him. I was hopeless at guessing ages, as I think most young people are. On reflection, though, I reckon they were in their early to mid thirties. I hit it off right away with Geoff and his wife Sheila and they agreed to let me stay for £5 a week, this would include all meals and pack ups.

After a few pleasantries, Des drove me to Mark's house so I could thank her for her hospitality and to pick up my gear. I was hoping to see Mark but he was already down the pub with his dad. Christ, I thought, that Mark's got hollow legs.

As soon as I got settled in at the Gough's house, it was late so I turned in. I slept like the proverbial log that night and was woken next morning by Geoff at the door with tea and toast. I was in total disbelief at the way I had been treated, both here and at Mark's home. If I had done to my room at home what I did to Mark's, well I dread to think what could have happened to me. Here also, are another couple of, virtual strangers treating me like I was their own son. Although my new base was some way away from the Shakespeare - my favourite boozer - it was on a bus route, so it would still be my local, for the time being anyway. So it was there that I headed after

tea from a jam jar   *Alfie Watson*

I'd had my first dinner with my new landlords.

    It was where all my mates and acquaintances hung out, so I was never lonely. There was always some of the gang in there, and we had some catching up to do, it was great. Arriving back at my new home, the Gough's were waiting to turn in. Saying their good-nights they gave me a key so they wouldn't have to stay up waiting for me in future. That suited me perfect, with never having had a key of my own at home, it felt strange though for someone who hardly knew me to be giving me so much trust. I knew we would get along fine.

Twenty-three

ICE CREAMS

April arrived and the long awaited ice cream job was just around the corner, so I caught up with Tommy and we arranged to meet Johnny Massarella at his depot. So he could introduce us to the horses and show us how to fit the harnesses and reigns etc. The first thing that surprised me was the size of these beasts. I don't know how many hands they measured but they towered over the pair of us. I couldn't help wondering what I was getting myself into. Once we'd managed to get the harness on and had fastened the horse to the cart, we were given some instruction on how to drive and steer. A couple of times round the yard was all we got, it seemed responsive enough, a tug on the right hand reign and it turned right and a tug on the left sent us turning left. 'Waugh there' made it stop and 'gee up' made it go. We were now fully trained horsemen! Johnny then introduced us to the freezer where the stock was kept, everything we needed for the day was either weighed or counted out and on return would be weighed and counted back, and our commission calculated. Well it all seemed straightforward enough so we agreed to turn up at 7am the following Saturday morning. I'd have to start to feign some sort of illness at work, on maybe Thursday or Friday so they wouldn't be so surprised at my absence on Saturday. I wasn't too concerned about the early

tea from a jam jar   *Alfie Watson*

start because I would have started at seven o'clock anyway if I had gone to work, but Tommy, well, he loved his bed. He didn't have a job so he had nothing to get up for normally, and used to just wake up nice and gently like nature presumably had intended. So it was quite a shock for him to find me banging on his door at six thirty. The rest of his family, which numbered three more brothers, all older than Tommy, and his mam, were not very pleased to be roused at such an ungodly hour. His dad had moved in with a woman four doors away but we never talked about him.

What appeared at the front door that morning was Tommy all right, but not the same one that I'd been out with just the previous night. He'd obviously been in some sort of a fight, but with who? He'd been with me most of the previous evening in the Shakespeare and he was fine then. One eye was closed completely and his nose looked like it might be broken. It was quite obvious that he was in a great deal of pain, as he descended the half a dozen steps from his front door, clutching at his ribs.' What the hell happened to you?' I asked. 'Bruno' he said, that fucking great ape in there. That's all he kept saying through the pain as we walked the couple of miles to the farm. I wondered if Johnny would let him take the cart out in that condition. By the time we arrived I'd found out what had happened to him.

He'd got home at about ten o'clock, after leaving me, to find Bruno on the settee. Presuming him to be asleep, he had started to remove some fags from his packet. The next thing he knew was Bruno's knee hitting him in the face and being

tea from a jam jar — Alfie Watson

sent sprawling into the dinner table, and to the floor. His mam, after hearing all the commotion, came to his rescue as his big brother pounded into him. I never did get to know his proper name, because Bruno was what everyone called him. He was the eldest of the four brothers and about ten years older than Tommy, he was a giant, built like the proverbial brick shit house, he used to demonstrate to anybody who'd watch, how he could lift a three foot by two foot council paving slab above his head with ease, and believe me, these things were seriously heavy. A fanatical body builder, he loved to show off his strength and seemed to take sustenance from knowing he was feared by all and sundry. It was said that his name had come from a comic character of the time. Everybody knew that he 'wasn't the full shilling.'

Johnny Massarella didn't even notice Tommy's condition, he was too pre-occupied with getting us sorted, or perhaps he did notice but felt some things were best left unsaid. After all, this was officially his first day in business, and he wanted those carts on the street no matter what. Our instructions were for one of us to operate on the Braunstone estate and the other on the New Parks estate, another council estate. It was decided that I'd take Braunstone. After much coaching in the techniques of making an ice cream cone and in particular the quantity to be given, we were let loose on the unsuspecting public.

I led the way down the long winding lane from the farm. The horses didn't need any help from us. As they trotted along I guessed they must have done this before. But this was their first day with me at the controls; I wondered how I'd cope at the main road, which was fast approaching. Waugh! Waugh! Waugh! I shouted, my voice getting progressively louder with each command, pulling as hard as I could on the reigns, I realised that it was obvious; we were not going to stop. This horse was out to play; after all it must have been a real treat to be let out of the field for a change, perhaps it would eventually settle down. I tugged on the right hand reign and we turned at great speed onto the main road, thankfully with no other traffic around, both carts made it safely. We now had a mile or so before the next obstacle; (a roundabout) so Tommy forgetting all his pain, decided we'd have a race. The road was narrow with room for one vehicle in each direction and for a big part of that mile we occupied both lanes as we jostled for the lead. Rather like a chariot race scene from Ben Hur, we hurtled along at what seemed like a hundred miles an hour. Luckily, like our trolley races years earlier, we didn't encounter any other traffic. I remember thinking; this was going to be great fun. At the roundabout we parted company, Tommy turned left and I went straight across, again without stopping or even slowing down. I was beginning to wonder if these animals were deaf, or perhaps just downright ignorant, after all, they responded to us all right at the rehearsals a few days earlier!

I headed for Braunstone as I had been instructed, but decided to err on the side of caution and kept the horse at a slow walking pace. That way it should be easier to stop when required, anyway it seemed a little more obedient now that it

tea from a jam jar — Alfie Watson

was on its own, it was probably just showing off to its pal. This 'it' that had given me so much trouble was in fact a female or a mare, as I would find out later. It seemed at the time, to be the right title for this headstrong animal. It was a word my mother was very fond of using when describing how the kids had behaved, on my dad's arrival from work. 'He or she's been an absolute mare today' or 'do you know what that little mare did today?'

The cart had only two wheels, taken; I was told from a defunct Austin seven, these were positioned at the point of balance. It had no windows, but had a large aperture at the front and one either side, with the entrance door at the rear so as you may well imagine, it was extremely draughty. Oh, and the horse provided the brakes, sometimes! We had a large brass bell that we used ring to attract customers, but rarely needed it as we naturally drew rather a lot of attention to ourselves, my mare and me as we entered the estate, and I was soon busy serving hoards of kids whenever I stopped. Such a sight had never been seen before and so far the horse was behaving herself, the exception being, when there was some nice long grass within eye-shot. Then she'd decide to move off, with the queue of customers in hot pursuit. I actually had to serve once, stranded in the middle of a traffic island. Looking back it must have been every ice-cream man's dream, to have customers running after him. Not all of them wanted to buy anything; some were only there to pick up the horse's droppings, apparently to put around the roots of their rose bushes.

tea from a jam jar   *Alfie Watson*

The sales were better than I could possibly have imagined, by lunchtime on that first day I'd started to run out of some things, such as lollies and ice cream tubs. But I still had plenty of loose ice cream to keep me going for a while. Unlike most ice cream vans, I ventured into streets and cul-de-sacs where there were no kids only the elderly, at first by mistake but then by choice. Here I found a wealth of custom just waiting for something to happen outside their windows, and an ice cream man was the perfect distraction from their otherwise mundane existence and a really big treat for them. Showing my soft side, as in the days at Miss Shipman's shop, I invited the old dears to bring a bowl and I would give them a few scoops and any trimmings they wanted just for the cost of a basic cone. The difference in this case was that It was my money that was paying for it. Nevertheless I got a great deal of satisfaction from seeing their grateful smiles.

The highlight on that first day, for me, came when I was parked not too far away from Tommy's house and working my way through the queue of, mostly kids, when Bruno turned up. Standing at the back, he was surrounded by kids, some tugging at his coat tails and others pleading for him to buy one for them. I thought night-time had come, as his gigantic frame reached the front of the queue sending the inside of the van into semi darkness. He, like many big men before him, had a soft side to his nature and ordered ice creams for about six kids and a big one with a flake for himself. It was at this stage that I got some retribution for what he'd done to Tommy the night before. With my back to him and the cone half filled I deposited a huge mouthful of spit right in the middle and topped it up with more ice cream and the flake. 'Enjoy' I said, as I handed it to him with a big smile. Tommy would have appreciated that and I couldn't wait to tell him, when we met up back at the depot. Johnny was more than pleased with our first day's sales and promised to give us extra stock the next day. Tommy was a bit miffed when he realised that I'd sold more than him, but the story about Bruno cheered him up! Relating the incidents of the day, we laughed all the way home.

Unfortunately all good things come to an end and Johnny had to take the vans off the road after only a few weeks, due to pressure from the Department of Health. Acting on complaints from members of the public, (more likely one our competitors) they had inspected the vans and had concluded that hand washing facilities should be installed in accordance with hygiene laws. Johnny duly obliged and both vans were fitted out before we took to the streets again. After a couple of weeks or so, another objection was raised, relating to the hygiene concerning the horses. Apparently a horse drawn ice cream van was not considered acceptable in respect to the animals toiletry needs. The proximity of certain parts of its anatomy in relation to the van and its contents also contravened several health and hygiene regulations.' What this really meant in plain English was, the horses arse was too close to the ice cream, and we were out of a job!

Well, it was fun while it lasted and we had many happy memories of those few weeks. Tommy's recollections about the time he had a dust up with one of the opposition ice cream men, was my favourite. He had been on his usual round during the second or third weekend when he had a close encounter with Mr Softy, who claimed that 'this was his patch.' Of course no one had any rights to any patch and Tommy had said so in no uncertain terms. The next couple of hours saw the vans leap frogging each other, each trying to be the first to reach new customers in the next street, often trying to anticipate where each other would be going to next. Not happy with this he decided to change tactics, now every time Tommy stopped; Mr Softy would park right in front of him. It must have been mayhem with Mr Softy playing his chimes and Tommy shaking his big brass school bell right behind. Although we always attracted lots of kids, they were mostly only interested in the horse, and anyway we were no match for this new type of soft ice cream. This competitor would have to be sent on his way soon or else most of the stock would be returned unsold, if it hadn't already melted before then. This new soft stuff was kept at a constant temperature by a refrigeration unit whereas our freezers, such as they were, relied solely on ice packs, similar to those used in today's cool boxes, only a lot bigger.

Word was sent ahead to Tommy's house that he was heading that way and needed some assistance. When he arrived outside, his three brothers were there to meet him. Jack, Mick and of course big bad Bruno, could always be relied upon when trouble was brewing and today was definitely going to be one of those days. Tommy filled them

tea from a jam jar   *Alfie Watson*

in with the details and they left, returning some minutes later with two large metal milk crates. Mr Softy man had arrived and was busy serving his way through a huge queue and didn't see the brothers until it was too late. Standing with their backs against the rear end of the van, their arms reaching down under the body, like three very large orang-utans, they lifted the van off the ground while Tommy slid the crates under the axles. With his competition well and truly out of action, Tommy went on his way.

From the police phone at the 'tardis,' situated only two hundred yards away, Mr Softy man reported his hijacking. Police enquiries later, drew a blank, with no one having witnessed the incident. Well, nobody was likely to name Bruno or his brothers were they? When he arrived back at the depot a couple of hours later, with his fridge completely empty, the police were there to greet him. The person they wanted to speak to was said to be 'in charge of a large brown horse pulling an ice-cream van'. There weren't too many of these about at the time. It was hard for him to deny the charges, but deny them he did, and he was eventually let off with a caution. Tommy found out later that it had taken a garage recovery team to rescue Mr Softy man, some two hours later.

Twenty-four

MOTORBIKES AND CARS

This strange but exciting chapter of our lives was slowly drawing to a close, with our interests now turning to the local youth club. This was held twice a week at the same school where my old mate Barry and I had attended the army cadets a couple of years earlier. Tommy had now acquired a motorbike, a Triumph Tiger cub, to be precise. I don't know if he had a license or even if he was insured, my guess was that he had neither. Anyway these things weren't necessary on private property so it wasn't an issue while we were there. With this 'mean' machine Tommy was always the centre of attention as far as girls were concerned, and he had them queuing up to get their leg over. The pillion that is!! He was a master of manoeuvrability and balance, and could ride along a given line almost at a standstill without deviation. The markings on the tennis court and netball pitch in the playground provided endless challenges for him, and I must admit he was pretty impressive to watch. It was on one of these visits to the youth club that I had my first experience of riding a motorcycle, A Triumph Tiger cub could never be considered a big or a powerful bike, but in the confines of a school playground with me in the saddle, it certainly felt like it. Having never even sat on one before, I was in need of a little tuition, which Tommy amicably provided. A crash

tea from a jam jar *Alfie Watson*

course was what I got, and crash is precisely what I did, and boy did I do it with style? My challenge was to try and ride along the straight line that marked the edge of the netball pitch without putting my feet down. Well, however hard I tried I couldn't keep the dammed thing steady, so Tommy suggested that I should open the throttle slightly. This I did and it was at this stage that I learned just how sensitive a motorcycle throttle could be. The bike surged forward with the back wheel flipping first to the left and then the right as I hurtled across the playground struggling to stay on board. I finally managed to get it under control to a degree but it was still going too fast and heading straight for the metal climbing apparatus. All I could think about was not smashing the bike up and I'm sure that was top of the list of Tommy's concerns as well, as he chased behind me, screaming for me to stop. Unfortunately I hadn't been shown how to do this on my brief training course, so my destiny and that of the bike was in the hands of someone upstairs. That someone, must have been my guardian angel because the bike went sailing right through this metal maize without making any contact whatsoever with only millimetres to spare on either side, leaving me winded and hanging like a rag doll over one of the horizontal bars. The bike continued across the playground for another thirty or forty yards, seemingly more under control now, where it came to a halt wedged inside a hawthorn bush. Luckily there was little or no damage done to the bike and we remained the best of pals.

Drinking in the Shakespeare one night I met up with Joe

again. He was now working for the water board and earning fabulous money. We sat chatting till closing time and arranged to meet up again the next day and over the next few weeks struck up quite a friendship. Some said we had become more like twins. We had the same taste in clothes and enjoyed dressing up a bit at the weekends. What a sight we must have looked as we strutted around the streets of the estate. Some might say that we looked like a couple of bookends, but did we care? No, of course not. We started to spend more time in the West end working men's club than in the Shakespeare, purely because the booze was a lot cheaper and they provided entertainment at weekends. Whenever I was with Joe I knew shit could happen and it nearly always did.

One night or maybe the early hours of the morning, we were heading from the club on our usual trip into town to get some food. On route, without any warning, he decided to dispense with his empty beer bottle straight through the plate glass window of an electrical store. My ability to run was called upon once again and this time we didn't stop until we reached the "Chuckie inn". This was where many teenagers gathered after a night out, sampling some of the greasy delights on offer. We joined the queue and ordered our usual chicken and chips. Now, instead of walking away from the scene of our earlier crime, we started to walk back towards it. Strolling casually along chatting and eating our supper, we didn't have a care in the world. Well that was all about to change! Stopping just inside a side street about fifty yards from the damaged window, we decided to have a piss up a wall. There we stood, with a chicken leg in our mouths and two streams of steaming piss heading for the curb, trying to deny to the police officers that we'd done it. They were obviously in the area because of the broken window , but it was never mentioned. Anyway we were both charged with causing a public nuisance and fined £10.

It was now New Years Eve and my resolution to stop drinking was already well on the way to being broken. Leaving the club with "auld Lang syne" still ringing in our heads, we made our way into town accompanied by a couple of bottles of Newcastle brown each. I remember that this winter of 1961 was bitterly cold with snow and ice a major problem. I think it started snowing in early December and by New Year the roads and pavements were still packed solid with ice. We stumbled and slid our way towards town, both totally rat-arsed, breaking and entering two or three houses or garages en route. I can clearly remember stealing a child's three wheel bike each and attempting to ride them into town. What a pair of tossers we must have looked. It never occurred to us that what we were doing was wrong and that it was so immoral to invade people's privacy the way we did, the thought of getting caught was never an issue. We thought we were untouchable and could get away with anything.

A few hundred yards further down the street Joe spotted a little white Thames van, not unlike the ones the water board used at that time. It was parked in the street, facing the opposite way to the way we were heading, with the keys in the ignition. It was too big a temptation for Joe, so before I

tea from a jam jar   Alfie Watson

could say, no Joe don't do it, he was in the driving seat with the engine running and raring to be off. I had little choice but to get in with him and to aid and abet another criminal act. He had no idea how to drive the bloody thing whilst sober never mind in this condition, although he reckoned the water board were teaching him, he couldn't even change gear so advised me that I should do it for him when he gave the nod. This was a perfect case of the pissed up blind leading the pissed up blind. Remarkably we managed to get the thing moving and negotiated the first junction with surprising ease and were now on a main road gradually increasing speed as his confidence grew. There was luckily very little traffic around due, I suppose to the lateness of the hour and also the conditions of the roads. Heading now for our first set of traffic lights with the packed ice glinting in the headlights, it dawned on me that he had no idea what he was doing. As he touched the brakes at the red lights we slid into the path of an oncoming car managing to avoid it by mere inches, we started to spin uncontrollably ending up with the car wrapped head on around a post box in a side street.

Both our heads smashed through the windscreen. Joe was slumped over the steering wheel with his glazed lifeless eyes, illuminated by the nearby street light, staring straight at me, with blood pouring from his face, I was scared. I was yelling at him to wake up at the same time as trying to open the passenger door. My beautiful white shirt was now blood red and I remember thinking this is getting serious as Joe suddenly lifted his head and attempted to drive off. I was now out of the car and wrenching at the buckled door on his side but it wouldn't open so he climbed over to my side and we legged it Joe going one way and me the other. I was amazingly only a couple of streets away from the Gough's, so I was off the street in a matter of minutes. All I could think of now was how bad my injuries were. Judging by the colour of my clothes, I was really expecting to be in a mess as I could still feel the warmth of the blood running down my face and neck. Letting my self in, I headed straight for the kitchen and washed in the sink, all the time waiting for the knock on the door from the police, which fortunately never came. With the help of lots of icy cold water the bleeding stopped and the damage was surveyed. The excessive bleeding was due to little splinters of glass from the screen that had left tiny cuts all over my head and forehead, and also from the fact that our blood was so full of alcohol, and therefore thin. All I had to do now was clean up the mess in the kitchen and dispose of my blood soaked clothes. These I pushed to the bottom of the dustbin. I really loved that suit but I knew it wouldn't be possible to get the blood out of it, anyway, I was alive, unhurt and still there'd been no knock.

New Year's Day started with breakfast in bed on a tray brought by Geoff. I don't know if this urge to eat a greasy breakfast after a session is peculiar to me but it really sets me up. I soon woofed that down and was up and ready to face another day, that, if circumstances had been slightly different, I might not have been having. Anyway after apologising for getting in late I was off up the club to see how Joe was. We had already agreed earlier that night that we would go back at dinnertime. I arrived at about 12 o'clock but there was no sign of him yet. When he finally arrived, about an hour later, I hardly recognised him. His right eye and the side of his face was very swollen and would without a doubt finish up with a hell of a shiner. That explains why I was unable to rouse him after the crash; he had knocked himself out either on the steering wheel, which had left terrible bruising to his chest, or the windscreen. Either way comparing us both I got off lightly, apart, that is for the loss of my precious suit. If the police had caught up with us, Joe would have had a hard time explaining where he had got those injuries. I couldn't help thinking I had a charmed life, and remember saying to myself, enough is enough, if I'm lucky enough to get away with this, I'm going to stay out of trouble for ever more. As it happened they didn't catch up with us and I didn't stay out of trouble. We parted on the understanding that we should not meet again until this blew over.

Twenty-five

BRAG

We were now growing up fast and we were becoming regular drinkers back at the Shakespeare spending a great deal of our time and money there, playing darts or cards with the locals. It soon became the meeting place for our gang from the estate. Enough time had passed and Joe and me were as one again. Gambling was not officially allowed in public houses, so when word had got around that the new publican at the Shakespeare was turning a blind eye, it attracted some seasoned card sharks from far and wide. At any given time there was about four or five card tables, all playing brag, with five or six players playing at each one. Other players would be hanging around waiting for their chance to sit in when a seat was vacated by someone who had probably just lost his wages, and now had to go and face his wife or mother! As is usual with card games, the stakes start off quite low and are civilised and friendly. Predictably as the night progresses and the beer flows, the stakes gradually get raised and the games become extremely serious. A hand that started with bets of a few shillings could quickly jump to pounds in a matter of minutes. It was Friday night, and with my pockets bulging I waited for a seat. I was eyeing one table in particular where Wayne- a severely handicapped wheelchair bound lad - was playing. There was some heavy betting going on between him and Joe with the kitty piled high with notes. The other two players were just making up the numbers, as is often the way.

Brag is a game where quite often the person with the most money will out bet his opponent regardless of how good their hand is. This was one such game. Two players, Wayne and Joe, were betting against each others hands and had reached the stage where they had both gambled a considerable amount without actually looking at their cards. This is known as going blind. If one player decides to look at his cards and wants to continue it will cost him double the other players stake each time he gambles. Joe was now getting low on funds so he decided to look at his cards. As the bet was already ten shillings (50 pence) blind, he knew that if he wanted to carry on it would cost him a pound. Whatever he saw in that hand, he made a decision to continue and played his money into the kitty. Wayne seeing that Joe's funds were low went for the jugular and raised the stakes to a pound blind.

A player who has seen his cards cannot conclude the game by asking to see a blind man's cards, but the player who has not, can. So the game will only reach a conclusion when the blind player asks to see the other players cards. Or one of them runs out of money. Joe was looking extremely nervous; his eyes flashing around at the crowd that always gathered with kitties this big, he searched his pockets, already aware that they were empty. He was looking for a way out of this mess and a friendly benefactor would do nicely. He only had enough cash for one more bet and he knew Wayne was sure to bet again. Either he had an unbeatable hand or he was feeling, that having bet so much already, he wasn't prepared give in to what was after all an unseen hand. Whenever I found myself in these situations and someone was prepared to bet everything on a hand that they, supposedly had not seen, I would have serious doubts about whether they had in fact had a sneaky look. And unless my hand was near to unbeatable, I would throw it in, (dack), cutting my losses and making sure that no one, playing or watching, saw what I was throwing away. So, although Joe was looking my way with an expression that said "lends a fiver", there was no way I would be doing that, even if he was a mate. Joe's face suddenly burst into a huge smile of relief as his "double" approached the table. Glancing at them both I realised I had just met his twin and he knew he'd found his lifeline. I was convinced now that he had a very good hand and so was Wayne. With the kitty at around forty pounds, there was only going to be one winner. With his brother's sponsorship, Joe was back in the driving seat and was about to put in another two pounds to continue, when the whole pub was thrown onto total darkness.

In the time it took for Wayne to fumble for the cycle lamp fixed to his wheelchair and illuminate the table, some opportunist had the audacity to pinch a handful of the kitty and was heading for the door about forty feet away. Joe, one or two others, and myself immediately gave chase while Wayne and his cronies watched over what was left of the cash. By this time cigarette lighters and matches had turned the room into something more resemblant of a nightclub, than a local pub bar. It was absolute bedlam as we raced towards

tea from a jam jar   *Alfie Watson*

the door through the crowded bar. Reaching the outside we found ourselves in total blackness, with the houses opposite in darkness and all street lights out, it was obviously a power cut that was affecting a large area. After a few seconds we managed to pick out the legs of someone running in the distance, picked out momentarily by the headlights of a car as it sped past. We gave chase and dragged him back to the pub, protesting his innocence all the way, and he may have been telling the truth because we couldn't find any money on him.

The inside of the pub had changed dramatically in the few minutes we'd been gone. It now resembled a western cowboy saloon. All the tables were now lit with candle light, courtesy of the landlord, as Wayne and his entourage awaited the arrival of our prime suspect. Whilst we really had no way of knowing whether this boy had anything at all to do with the missing money, we did want to know why he was running away. Still proclaiming he'd done nothing wrong, we dragged him sobbing to face the music.

He was very smelly and scruffy in appearance, aged about fifteen years old. He had, sometime in the past, sustained serious burns to his face and I couldn't help noticing that he was severely cross-eyed. What a pathetic specimen he portrayed and I for one began to feel just a little bit sorry for him. Some one in the pub said they knew him, and that his family were new to the estate. New they maybe, but this didn't seem like the best way to introduce yourself to the people gathered around this particular table. After a good deal of interrogation he finally broke down and confessed at the same time pulling the money from his underpants. This gives credence to one of my mother's favourite sayings about, "never putting money in your mouth". He'd managed to grab about six pounds and I thought he would be beaten to within an inch of his life. With the money now safely back in the kitty it was decided to finish the hand of cards before dealing with him.

When he'd given chase, Joe had the presence of mind to take his cards with him. So Wayne could still have no idea what the strength of his hand was, but still, it was Joe who suggested that the game be abandoned and the cash shared between the only two players left. This prompted accusations that he was looking for a way out of a hand that he never had a chance of winning. Of course he had held the winning hand before the lights went out, but he had also left the table and the pack of cards unattended for quite some time. He also knew that he couldn't suggest directly that there'd been cheating going on, or there might have been two beatings that night! Although it had got extremely heated at one stage, eventually the game was wound up and everyone remained on friendly terms, and right on cue, the lights came back on. What happened next was quite amazing given the seriousness of what had taken place earlier. Because Wayne was severely disabled, he was always accompanied by two or more heavies, especially around the card table, where violence had a habit of erupting. But here was this man - who often ordered his henchmen to beat up people just for looking at him - showing such humility and kindness towards this boy, this stranger. He showed us all a compassionate side of him that none of us had ever witnessed before, immediately striking up an affinity with him, which would last for many years. Although I never found out the boy's name, I had to admire his guts in doing what he did that night and I feel sure this is what attracted Wayne to him. Or did the fact that he was disfigured have more to do with it?

Sadly, Wayne was to become extremely depressed in later life and ended it all with a bullet.

What had happened that Friday night was the topic for discussion for weeks after, and as I'd suspected, it was pretty likely that Joe had held the winning hand. One Two Three on the bounce was the hand, on the bounce meaning the cards were all the same suit. In the game of three card brag, there is only one hand that could beat this, and it was unlikely that Wayne had got it. Well not by honest means anyway!

Twenty-six

A CLOSE SHAVE

Joe and I were slowly becoming real mates, the sort who would see each other every day. Getting into trouble was the norm. There was never any nasty violence, we were just being stupid and pushing our luck. In a particularly boisterous mood one night, in the middle of a darts match, I decided to remove the light bulb from it's socket, plug in my razor and proceed to have a shave. As it turned out, it was a very close shave, not because of anyone in the home team; they saw the funny side of it. No it was the away side that kicked off. Well looking back I doubt whether I would have liked it much either. They were in the middle of a crucial game of darts, (they were all crucial) when this tall lanky dick head parks a bar stool right in the middle of the ockey and starts having a shave. I would have gone ballistic. There were some very big men in that team who knew how to handle themselves, and they were becoming very agitated. Whilst we and the home side thought it was hilarious, there was an atmosphere slowly building. Promising that I wouldn't be too long now I thought I could keep them at bay and I did to an extent. The trouble really started when, after finishing my shave, I put the bulb back in and it didn't work. Then it started, the away side began pushing and shoving, we shoved back and the home team pushed with us. Then the sound of breaking glass as a table got knocked over. If I remember correctly all eight of the home team, which included Joe's twin brother, were helping us ward off about four or five of the away side, so it was always going to be no contest. Plus, there were, I don't know how many locals in the pub who would have come to our aid. It was a kind of territorial thing. Anyway with the sound of the breaking glass, came the landlord and his biggest barman, who'd been busy preparing the after match supper. The match had been nearing the end and they were playing what's known as the beer leg. Our interruption was perfectly timed as it so happened, because the Shakespeare boys were losing and nobody liked losing the beer leg because they would have to buy the winners a drink each. Anyway all this disruption meant that the post match supper possibly being served dry and overcooked. The end result was that we were both barred from using the pub again. Not surprising though, given the facts, the landlord hardly had any choice. We left the pub more than a little worse for wear and decided that we couldn't be bothered to walk home. Outside in the pub yard, leaning against the wall were two mopeds. As if by telepathy we selected one each and off we went on our merry way. Taking a longer route than we would normally have, had we been walking, we were being seen by many people who used the pub. This was to be our downfall. Leaving my bike some way away from my digs so not to draw attention to myself, I thought I had committed the perfect crime.

    The next day after having dinner with the Gough's I was on my way out of the front door, to go and meet up with Joe again, when I noticed some one I knew from the Shakespeare. Could this be the owner of the moped, I thought. He was casually leaning against the wall of a house opposite. Reversing swiftly back inside and slamming the door shut behind me, I had this overwhelming urge to use the toilet. I knew now what it meant when people said they were so scared, they were shitting themselves. The Gough's never suspected anything untoward, but they would have done if I'd stayed in and watched the telly with them. Since moving in, I had never stopped in, although I'd stopped out a few times. I got away from there eventually by using an alley at the back of the house that ran the complete length of the street. An alley that my adversary didn't seem to know existed.

For the next two days every time I tried to leave the house at night, he was there. If he hadn't been 100% sure that I was the culprit, then I'm sure he was now and he wasn't going to give up until he got his revenge. I knew that I couldn't keep leaving the house this way, without the Gough's getting suspicious, up to now they had no idea what was going on. Luckily the sitting room in these terraced houses was at the back; otherwise they would have also spotted him loitering around. I knew that one day I would have to face him so I made my mind up, it was to be tonight. I was absolutely terrified after all, this was a man in his late thirties and I was a mere boy. There was no way on earth that I was even going to fight back, I deserved what was coming, in any case I knew his family and they had a reputation for violence. Trust *me* to nick *his* moped! Well, this was it; I'd spent all day preparing

tea from a jam jar   *Alfie Watson*

myself, thinking that if I did present myself to him, then it could all end with just a stiff talking to. As I headed towards my fate my bowels were on the move again, I'm thinking all sorts of things, the last thing I wanted to do was shit myself in front of him. So after visiting the toilet for the third or fourth time since arriving from work, I was opening the door to face my fate. Imagine my surprise when I realised he wasn't there. The pressure was gone; it was like someone had lifted a ton of bricks from my shoulders. He must have given up on me because he had been there about an hour earlier because I had seen him as I peeped from behind the net curtains in my bedroom. This was confusing because I knew he would not give up easily, it was not the way things happened with these people. Had he decided to tell the police and let them deal with me? No that's not their way either, or perhaps he'd nipped to the shops for fags, had he gone home ill or to get re-enforcements to watch the back gate? All these things were racing through my mind, I would have preferred for him to have been there and I could have got it over and done with, this was torture. As I headed down the road towards the bus stop where I got the bus to the estate, I was expecting him to jump out of every alleyway I passed. I'm imagining what I would have done in a similar circumstance and I know I wouldn't have waited directly outside the house; it would have been more of a shock, were I to leap out and surprise him totally. His way of dealing with me was probably the more affective because I knew why he was there and he knew that I knew. I also had a pretty good idea what the end result would be; he was getting a kick out of making me sweat.

tea from a jam jar — Alfie Watson

Well, I had walked passed about ten alleys or entries and he still hadn't announced himself, yet he's had loads of opportunities. With about 50 yards to go I was feeling safe, with the corner at the end of the street fast approaching I held my breath in anticipation. As I turned the corner I was hit in the stomach with what felt like a knee, and immediately fell to the floor, instinctively curling up into the foetus position. The punches and kicks rained in on me accompanied by expletives and warnings about even thinking about doing anything like this again and let this be a warning, don't mess with me again. As quick as it had started, it was over and he'd gone, and I had indeed been given a lesson. I couldn't help thinking that had he caught up with me sooner, the beating would probably have been a lot worse. Anyway battered and relieved that it was now all over and done with, I caught the bus to Braunstone and met up with Joe. I couldn't wait to see how he'd got on, because misdemeanour's such as this, on the estate, were always settled in this way. But he looked fine, not a mark on him. Perhaps they hadn't found him yet and he still had his beating to come.

As we headed off towards the West end club, where, at least I knew I wouldn't meet my attacker, he tells me that the bike I thought he'd pinched, had in fact, belonged to his brother, who was in the darts team that night, and he'd told him he could borrow it. Naturally he thought it was hilarious.

We often had girls hanging around when we were loitering around the shops at night time but we were not interested in them apart from the odd bit off groping in the shop doorways.

tea from a jam jar   *Alfie Watson*

These girls loved the attention they were getting and just drifted around the group getting their sexual thrills, we weren't doing too badly either. There were a couple in particular who didn't mind what we did or where we did it. One, known by the lads as Cutty, I don't know why, was up for any thing and was at her happiest when she had two lads to fondle and she was getting her thrills in duplicate. We had our favourite places to take her but usually it would be the toilet on the park after closing time. All the park gates would be locked at around eight o'clock in those days. That's when we seemed to use the park the most. It wasn't difficult to find a way in, often by just bending the iron fence and squeezing through. We would find ourselves with Cutty, either laying on the grass or standing up in the toilets. She absolutely encouraged us, one would be fondling here tits and she was very well endowed, whilst the other played with her fanny. After so long we'd swap ends, whilst she would keep a firm grip on our cocks until we were both satisfied. We would then disappear to the Shakespeare leaving her there in the dark to get dressed.

    She was always back the next night with no complaints, and as obliging as usual. I had always had this image of her marrying into a harem where endless sex was almost guaranteed. This girl was always available and I can never remember her saying no. Although, on reflection I can't say I can remember asking her for sexual favours anyway, it was almost as if she felt it was her duty, this is why she was on this earth. Even when she was having a period she would still

tea from a jam jar   *Alfie Watson*

be available, I think she mainly enjoyed having her tits played with and on these occasions we were allowed to shag the tops of her thighs. She was without doubt the best of all the girls and quite pretty with it. The others sort of provided back up in case Cutty was otherwise engaged, they could never compete with her. Some of them had hardly any tits so didn't like you to touch them there but were absolutely gagging to be fingered and shagged so we couldn't let them down. What we got up to with these girls was the prelude to the night, after which we'd be up the pub. On reflection they were extremely good times.

Twenty-six

I MEET KAREN

Through the jungle telegraph I heard that my big sister Sue had got wed at the registry office to a boy named Colin, who I'd never heard of until now. Apparently he was taken there in handcuffs because he was serving a prison sentence for robbery. There was still a few more weeks of his sentence left to serve. Like me she was looking for a way to get away from that house, and jumped at the first bloke who came along. I didn't go to the wedding, I wasn't invited, but then neither was anyone else. It was a registry office wedding done as cheap and as quickly as possible because we found out later that she was up the duff. Not the ideal start to married life but then compared to the alternative, she obviously thought it was her best option. There would be no way she would be able to stop at home in that condition. She was wed for about six months before Colin was arrested again for robbery with violence and was eventually sent down again, this time it was to be for four years. This was a terrible blow to poor Sue and divorce was not far away from her mind. He was serving his time in Wakefield prison while Sue struggled to bring up her first child. From the frying pan into fire comes to mind.

A police officer told Sue on one of her visits to see Colin that she was to tell me that they had their eyes on me and it was only matter of time before they would get me. I knew

tea from a jam jar *Alfie Watson*

that I was pushing my luck and I couldn't keep getting away Scot free. But it may also have been a little white lie by her to get me to sort myself out. Well it soon became obvious to everyone who knew us that Joe and me would end up like Colin, in prison, and the next incident convinced me that enough was enough. I will not write anything relating to this in this diary, other than to say that it was a very serious and a very real scare and maybe just what I needed, the message from Sue just reinforced what I had been thinking for a while. I had to stop seeing Joe.

I bumped into Mark; I hadn't seen him for a while so we had a couple of beers and chatted. It turns out he's only gone and got himself a car, yet I didn't know he was even having driving lessons. A black Austin A40 bought for him by mummy. Well, he was off out in it that night and I was invited to join him. He picked me up at my digs and headed for the Braunstone estate, telling me we were heading for the West end working men's club. Well it was not the way I would have gone but hey it's his car and I thought he was just taking a longer route to show off. Pulling up outside a house in the middle of the estate he then explains that he's picking a bird up. Minutes later this tall gorgeous brunette walked towards the car. No way, I remember thinking, she can't be going out with Mark, never in a million years. Mark was a nice guy but good looking, he most certainly was not. I was in the front passenger seat as he reached over to open the door; I had my first close up of her. It had to be the car that had pulled her; she was much too pretty to be seen with him. I began chatting to her as soon as she climbed aboard and after a couple of minutes reached slyly behind my seat and held her hand. I was smitten with this girl, never mind brown eyed handsome man - a Buddy Holly song around at that time - this was one brown eyed beautiful girl. When we reached the club Mark treated her as a trophy and paid her very little attention, in fact I think he was at the bar more than he was with her. I didn't mind, it gave me a chance to chat her up and I didn't waste any time doing that. It was Friday and I knew Mark would be drinking with his dad as he did every Saturday and Sunday lunch time. So I arranged to meet her at the Braunstone Victoria club, the place that had provided all the victims of mine and Barry's antics around the lamppost years earlier.

We met that Saturday lunchtime and we got on really well, I was besotted, her name was Karen and she was fifteen years old and I was eighteen. She was one of a family of fourteen and I was one of eleven, she was not happy at home and I certainly wasn't, that's why I was in digs, so we had a lot in common straight away. I was due to meet her again the next night on a street corner and maybe we'd just walk and talk, I hadn't made any real plans to do anything special. I didn't mind because as long as she was with me she couldn't see Mark as she'd planned to do. He'd get over it!

I went to see Sue and my new niece whom they'd named Linda. I couldn't stop talking about this beautiful girl I had met, so she suggested we baby sit for her that night and I agreed. But on the way back to my digs I was having serious doubts about what Karen might think about such a suggestion on our first real date. So next morning I decided to catch a bus up to Braunstone and arrived at her front door unannounced. This was a shit hole of a place from the outside but when the door opened, it was clear that the inside wasn't a great deal better. One of her brothers answered my knock and called out her name. After observing an assortment of strange shaped heads peeking at me from the inner rooms, she finally arrived at the door. Her hair was a mess, she had no make-up or shoes on and was wearing a tatty looking overcoat which doubled as a dressing gown. She had obviously just got up and was surprised to see me standing there and somewhat embarrassed that I'd caught her looking like this. This would not have happened today as I would have simply called her on her mobile. It didn't matter to me what she looked like that day, I knew what she looked like the day before.

  I couldn't get her out of my mind, those big brown eyes and her ruby red lips, tall and slim, with gorgeous legs she could easily have been a model. Any way she agreed to baby sit with me but did not want to be out too late as it was work the next day and she had to be there for 6am, walking all the way, a distance of about 4 miles. The baby sitting was a success and Sue liked her immediately. We saw each other regularly after that date and the more I saw her the more I liked her. I began to find out more about her background, such as how her dad was hardly ever at home for them. He would always go straight on the booze as soon as he finished work and often wouldn't get home till the pubs shut, that was

tea from a jam jar   *Alfie Watson*

10 o'clock then. Sometimes he would not arrive home until the early hours of the next morning, this would be because he'd sometimes go for a meal with his drinking buddies. This was his routine and and had been for many years, often beating her mother if she dared to say anything about his behaviour.

The Catholic Church played a big part in Karen's upbringing, regularly providing food and clothing in the absence of any wages, which had been frittered away on booze and gambling. She would often recall how she and her sister were sent to wait outside his watering hole (pub) in order to get some money from him before the bookmaker did. This was deprivation not only of love but also food and clothing. I knew my dad was a bastard towards me in particular and was often out of work but compared to what Karen had to deal with, mine was a cosy life. She always looked and smelled gorgeous often wearing home made clothes, something she had taught herself to do at an early age.

Some of the stories she shared were a testament to her determination to survive. Stories of how, when younger, she would sometimes buy an egg, rather than sweets with any money she would acquire because she was so hungry. The neighbours were also aware of the plight of the family and used to pass left over food over the fence. She must have been worried sick, knowing that one day she would have to ask me to meet her parents, well that day had arrived and I was extremely nervous myself at the prospect, especially of meeting her dad. His reputation had gone before him and it frightened the hell out of me. One story I had heard was that, whilst he was making his way home one drunken night, a snappy little Jack Russell dog was trying to take lump out of his leg. The dog followed him and tested his patience until he finally cracked and grabbed the dog, biting it as hard as he could. The dog, so the story goes, ran off yelping and never bothered him again.

I needn't have worried because it was late when we got to her house and he was sprawled out in an armchair his legs outstretched and fast asleep. So my first meeting with her dad looked like it would have to be postponed. After the introductions, her mother said her good nights and left the room only to return a couple of minutes later to strategically place an empty bucket on the floor between his outstretched legs, she gave a little chuckle and left the room. I looked on in absolute amazement, not knowing what was going on. I had presumed this was just a bit of a laugh. Some time later as we cuddled on the settee, I should say, cuddled on the springs on the settee, it started. Her dad pissed himself in his sleep, most of the urine went into his trousers and the chair, but some found its way into the bucket. Shortly after this I made my excuses and left, more to protect Karen from any further embarrassment than anything else.

Can the reader possibly begin to imagine how humiliating this must have been for Karen? I was determined that this incident would not effect my relationship with her, although it was a long time before I would be invited into the house again. I couldn't help thinking what a mismatched couple they were, he was an absolute giant of a man, weighing in at around 20 stone and standing about 6 feet tall, she on the other hand was a small fragile looking lady with dark unkempt hair with a mouthful of bad or broken teeth probably weighing in at around five stone.

Shortly after we met, Karen changed her job and was now working in the hosiery, with an 8 o'clock start. In fact the bus she used to catch would pass by the factory window at around 7.45 every morning and I was always looking to catch a glimpse of her on the upper deck, and would encourage anybody who was around to have a look. Sadly, I never actually saw her, partly because the bus flashed by too fast and also because she always sat on the same seat and that was out of our view. I did think one day that I spotted her legs. How besotted was I? The blokes at work were getting sick and tired of hearing me going on about her. They could tell how this girl was affecting me and I was constantly being teased that I would soon be married, my response was always the same, no way!!

It would soon be her birthday and she wanted a hair-drier, I seemed to remember her saying she had one but it was bought from a rummage sale and wasn't a lot of good. With the hair-drier I also bought a record, it was Brenda Lee and the song was "as usual". I knew she had a record player of some sort, but I wasn't sure how good it was. It soon transpired that the record player- also from a rummage sale- was a really old one, so old, it had to be wound by a handle. So I bought her a

tea from a jam jar   *Alfie Watson*

state of the art Decca electric one.

    We were seeing an awful lot of each other now. One weekend I took her to the Shakespeare for a couple off drinks. We were sitting outside, as the weather was gorgeous, just chatting and enjoying each others company, when trouble arrived in the form of six or seven local youths. I knew some of them, especially the leader and knew instantly that they had not come for a chat. They approached very slowly and menacingly then one by one they sat down as close as they could get to us, all the time taunting me and looking and waiting for a response. When none was forthcoming, the ring leader picked up my glass and drank the small amount of beer that was left, before placing the empty glass back down in front of me. That would normally have been my cue to lash out. But what I did, surprised even me, I took Karen by the hand and led her away without saying a word. This was the first time I had ever reacted like this when confronted, But it didn't feel good, and as we walked hesitantly away, I was already plotting my revenge. It was the ring leader who I was planning to meet, the bastard who had the nerve to drink my beer and humiliate me in front of the person I cared the most about in the whole world. I think that even if there had only been one of them that day, I would have still reacted the same way, because I was changing, by that I mean I was growing up at last and felt a certain protectiveness for Karen; she was after all, having more than enough aggravation at home, without me providing more. I knew where this guy lived and made it my priority to see him on his own.

tea from a jam jar   *Alfie Watson*

I went to his home purporting to be a friend and his mother said he would be home from work at around 5.30pm, so I waited by the gate, hidden from the house by privet, but able to see both ends of the street. Sure enough he turned the corner bang on time, but as soon as he got close and spotted me, he legged it, I waited for about an hour before giving up for the day, satisfied that at least he would be late for his tea and I knew I would be back tomorrow and the next day until I got him. I knew now which way he approached the house so I could hide myself away ready to pounce. He walked right into my trap this time but managed somehow to run back to the front gate before I launched a barrage of punches and he just squealed like a girl, so loud it brought his mammy to his side. I left him in her arms. He wouldn't bother me again.

We were living in extraordinary times. The sixties were good years, although we didn't realise quite how good at the time. The Beatles had just hit the scene with their first number one hit "please please me". National service had been abandoned, so luckily I missed the call up, which would've meant two years in the army. No longer my chosen profession now that Karen was in my life. Transistor radios were just coming on the scene. A Russian had become the first man into space. Mary Quant was top designer. The mini was the first small car. Life was good.

One of my problems then and some may say still is, was my inability to control my temper. At work, we were getting quite a lot of poor quality raw materials (yarn). It was obviously being bought in cheaply. The plan was that it would be rewound and all the imperfections would be removed. Unfortunately this became impractical because the yarn could not be processed quickly enough to supply the knitting machines that needed it. Leaving some of us having to contend with the unwound yarn and all the problems it caused. Because our work was piece work based, in other words our earnings depended on what we produced, this soon affected our wages. This led to some people hoarding and hiding the rewound yarn. Some even started to arrive at work extra early in order to stock pile and then stay at their machines during the break periods to guard their stash. The days when we would all gather in the toilets first thing and have a fag and a natter, were now long gone. All the camaraderie has gone and it's not so much fun as it used to be.

It's Monday morning, I'm late and nursing the mother of all hangovers. All the best yarn had already been secreted away before I arrived, so I didn't get off to a very good start and things were about to get worse. In a fit of rage after one of these unwound yarn cones had caused an horrendous mess of the knitting head, which would take me ages to repair, I finally cracked and lost my temper, picking up the two kilo cone I threw it down the room through a plate glass window. It was an extremely stupid and childish thing to do as this window, about 20 feet away, was directly above the entrance to the building. Luckily for me most people had arrived for work, or I could have been in serious trouble as somebody could have easily been badly injured or worse. I made no attempt to fix the machine, or clear away the broken glass, knowing It wouldn't be too long now until the foreman, Walter, would arrive at the end of my ally, as he did every morning. He would always stand at the end of each alley in turn, to ask what work tickets we required. Well, he stood there waiting with his pen and clipboard at the ready but his attention was soon diverted by the draught blowing right at the back of his head. Who's done this? "I fucking did, it's where that shit you call yarn belongs."

His starched bleached white collar emphasised the bright red colour of his face as he stormed off back to his office, but I knew he'd soon be back. I could just see his arm and a phone in his hand from my alley, obviously he was taking advice on how to deal with this situation. All the blokes I worked with knew what I had to contend with, they wouldn't use the unwound yarn simply because it was rubbish. But I didn't expect any support or sympathy from them because what I did was stupid and downright dangerous to anyone who had the misfortune to be entering the building at that particular time. I didn't have to wait long as he marched up the ramp that led to my set of machines; he had that look of a man on a mission. I think his words were, get your tools and your coat and leave the building now, you're fired. I wasn't particularly concerned as things had been getting me down for a long time so it was something of a relief to be walking out and knowing that I would never have to face all the crap any more.

In those days the hosiery trade was booming so I knew that

tea from a jam jar — *Alfie Watson*

I wouldn't be out of work for long. I was out looking for work the very next day, and it wasn't long before I landed another knitting job for double the pay. There was a slight downside to it though, it was shift work and I'd never done anything other than day work, so this could be interesting. I knew it wouldn't be much of a wrench to leave my so called mates; after all, they were only interested in themselves. It was, I suppose understandable as they were mostly young married men now with families depending on them and big mortgages to pay. Here was a group of good men who used to be so united and even militant on occasions, being split apart by the need to provide for their families and a managements determination to divide and rule. Boy was I relieved to be free from that rat race. I didn't realise at the time but I was heading straight into another that would prove to be just as bad.

My first taste of shift work was a bit of a shock to my system on several fronts. Firstly the early shift started at 6am, meaning I'd have to be up at about 5 and I knew this when I took the job, but I hadn't realised just how early 5am was. Well that's the time I set my alarm for, but it was more like a quarter to six when I'd get up. At first I would leap out of bed, more or less straight onto my bike and pedal like mad, no wash, no food, just my pack up, and get there a few minutes late. This did not meet the approval of the bosses and I was warned that if my time keeping didn't improve, I'd be looking for another job. To make matters worse, they also made it clear that, although the early shift started at 6am, they

tea from a jam jar   Alfie Watson

expected me to be there at least 10 minutes earlier, to achieve a smooth changeover from the night shift. In order for me to get up at such an unholy hour, I decided that I would have to be in bed by about 9pm. It worked fine for a while but I gradually slipped back into my old ways. I was fine with nights and the late shift; I just hated this early start. The bosses in their wisdom came up with a plan to encourage better time keeping.

I wasn't the only one; there were possibly two or three of us who could be classed as regular offenders. Each knitter would have his own knitting machines to operate, so three of us were responsible for making sure that this particular set of machines ran around the clock daily, working eight hours each. The rule was that anyone who did not arrive and clock in before 6.30am, the set of machines they were due to operate would be shared out amongst the other knitters. A set consisted of four machines so consequently an extra machine added to each knitter set meant that the operators would be earning considerably more pay on that day, as with my previous job, we were paid on what was produced. Well, although I tried really hard to get up, there were the odd days when, for whatever reason I would be late. The entrance to the factory was at the rear, by way of a cul-de-sac. As I turned the corner I could see my so called work mates lined up at the windows, their hands on their brows and pressed against the glass as if gazing into the sunset; instead they were staring into the darkness, hoping and praying that I wouldn't make it in time. So here again we had a case of the bosses attempting to divide us.

On the occasions when I was late I would be given some poxy menial job to do such as sweeping the floor or cleaning windows, with wages to match. It was a smart move by the bosses and a good incentive for me to try harder, which I did and my time keeping improved significantly. At least with this shift, along with nights, I could see Karen for a couple of hours a day but the late shift meant that we couldn't see each other for a week, and that was a real killer. A proportion of the wage was made up with an amount which was called unsociable earnings; well I knew exactly what they meant by that now!

I was now back at home with my parents, tempted back more because I wanted to be nearer to Karen than any other reason. Geoff, my landlord could not cope with the strange hours I was now keeping and asked me to look for somewhere else. Also as a lodger, I didn't feel I could doss around the house, on my spare time, like perhaps I could at my own house, although I doubt that would be pleasant either. He was a great bloke and both he and his missus really looked out for me as if I was one of their own, I would miss them more than they would miss me. I doubt I'll be getting a hot meal on arriving home from work or packed lunches any more, that was for sure. I am absolutely positive that I would not have been welcomed back home if it wasn't for the fact that they had now lost Sue's board money. I was purely a means to an end.

tea from a jam jar   *Alfie Watson*

The shift work meant that I was at home when the house was quiet, the kids were at school, and dad was at work so life was quite a lot better. I rarely saw him any more and that suited me fine. When I was on the early shift, I'd be long gone (providing I managed to get up) before he was up. On the late shift he would be in bed by the time I got home and when I was on nights I would usually be out somewhere when he would get home and in bed the next morning before he was up. So, yeah it was working out quite well.

They did stipulate that I could not go back and pay the same board money, as I was now earning more than when I left and It didn't seem to be negotiable, My dad was asking for double what I was paying before I left and that was £5 a week then. I was going around with mates like Mark who were not paying a penny.

Twenty-seven

BULLY OF A FATHER

So I stood my ground and the final arrangement was that I would pay £5 as before and would still have to pay for any baths I had, by putting however much was needed in the gas meter. I was also expected to contribute to the cost of the Sunday joint every week now and not just occasionally as before. Geoff and his wife charged me five pounds a week and threw in a smile and loads of hospitality for free. I had been home for a few weeks now without incident and was having a lay in, when I was shouted from my bed. One of Karen's brothers had arrived on the doorstep with news that Karen was in hospital. I can't remember getting dressed so quick since the early days of my shift work.

Arriving at the hospital, it turns out that she'd taken an overdose. Things had reached breaking point at home when her mam and dad were having a blazing row which ended in her mam suffering yet another beating at the hands of this bully. Karen had responded bravely by picking up the first thing at hand and stabbing him in the back. Luckily for both of them, that this thing was a fork, picked out of the kitchen sink. The worrying thing was that it could easily have been a carving knife. Anyway it was enough to distract him but he then turned his attention to Karen, who, after receiving a couple of side swipes from him, fled to her bedroom and

tea from a jam jar   *Alfie Watson*

gulped down a handful of phenobarbetone anticonvulsants. These were in the house because her older sister, Christine suffered from epileptic fits from time to time. The treatment at the hospital for an overdose then, and probably still is today, was a stomach pump. A pipe being pushed down the gullet into the stomach and the contents pumped out. She looked terrible and really sickly, but she was allowed to go home within a couple of hours of this procedure. The nurses had not made her time there a comfortable one, being extremely judgemental without first learning the facts. If this had happened today, I'm sure she would have had to see a councillor, who probably would have involved social services and they in turn would arrange a home visit. From this they would see first hand that her mam was badly bruised and needed protection from any further abuse from this monster, and they would also be made aware that some of the children were extremely under nourished and generally neglected. But this was then, and society was not quite as protective of its children as it is today.

Arriving back at her house from the hospital, Karen suggested that I should leave her at the front door because she wasn't sure how either of us was going to be greeted. I was terrified at the thought of facing her dad, but I had to stand up to him even if it meant that I would have to run like a whippet afterwards. I remember Karen going to bed immediately we entered the house. I opened the door to the front room where I was about to confront him, leaving the doors open behind me in case I needed to make a quick exit. Sure enough, there he sat in the urine soaked chair he was in when I had first set eyes on him a few weeks earlier. I can't remember my exact words to him, but it was something like: I suppose you're proud of yourself are you? I could now feel my legs starting to shake, betraying my brave words. As his huge hands slammed down on the arms of the chair, he started to raise himself up. Seeing that I was standing my ground he sunk back down again, I took this opportunity to warn him not to touch her again, as I reversed slowly from the room, my heart pounding like a drum inside my chest.

I am not so stupid as to think he was afraid of me on that day, but I am sure he was surprised at my defence of his daughter and this seemed to earn me his respect. To my knowledge he never touched her or her mother again. I was invited to go back to the house many times after this and he accepted me like a son.

Eventually, after several weeks, me and her dad had bonded enough to share a couple of pints in the local boozer. I was aware that he was a big time drinker and I was a mere novice by comparison. My first trip out with him was to the Shoulder of Mutton, the nearest pub, and conveniently situated on the estate, two streets away. With his reputation foremost in my mind we set off for my first visit to this extremely notorious establishment. This place was filthy; the bar was swimming with beer slops as were the tables and floor. Men still in their work clothes were gathered around tables where card schools were in progress. Others grouped around the dart board, the air thick with tobacco and pipe smoke. This sort of bar was

tea from a jam jar
Alfie Watson

pretty normal for these times, but this was the roughest one I had ever been in. Several dogs, some mongrel's and a couple of Jack Russell's were roaming around sniffing and licking the soaking wet floor. I actually watched one of the mongrels piss up the leg of an unsuspecting drinker as he leaned on the bar chatting to a mate. Charlie, as I was now allowed to call him, was first to the bar and ordered two pints of mild; this was the tipple of the working man back then. I did so much want to impress, so with my first swig, my glass was half empty as I proudly placed it on the table at the side of his, which had about half an inch sipped from it. Some big drinker he is, I thought, as I emptied my glass with my second swig. With empty glass in hand I made my way back to the bar. Same again mate? Said the barman with a big wide grin. Yes please I said, my chest puffed out with pride. Returning to the table with two more pints, it became clear that this was not the contest I thought it was going to be. There he sat this big bruiser of a man, with a drinking pedigree to match, still not even a quarter the way through his first pint. I was leaving him standing and his pints were lining up. But then, rather like a marathon runner, without any warning his pace increased and he started to work his way through them with consummate ease as the barman's grin grew wider. As the night went on, the more I became aware that this was a classic hare and the tortoise situation with me being the hare. By the end of our session I was talking double Dutch and seeing double whilst he was just knocking back doubles. When we left I was virtually unable stand, let alone walk and my pockets were empty, whereas he seemed as sober as a judge and he'd downed, I don't know how many whiskeys while he waited for me to catch up. I couldn't help wondering how much it would cost for this huge man to get so drunk that he would need to be brought home by his drinking buddies, pretty much every night of the working week. How much to get him so drunk that he had to be left on the doorstep of his house some nights, because he was too heavy for them to get him inside? He would lay there till he sobered up, sometimes until daybreak, but not before his wife had emptied his pockets.

What a selfish bastard he was. His family were on the poverty line; relying on handouts from the neighbours and the local Catholic Church to survive, and here he was pissing every penny he earned up the wall not to mention the money spent in the bookmakers. Later in his life, when terminal illness took over him, it was noticeable that his wife showed little compassion or concern. Was this her time for retribution? I think possibly it was.

Karen and myself were becoming closer than ever, I suppose partly due to the fact that I was now more aware of all the suffering she must have endured while growing up in that house. It was never sympathy that I felt but more admiration that she could spend her life in such deprivation and yet be so immaculately turned out whenever we met. We were now taking every available opportunity to be together. We decided to start meeting when I was working the late shift from 2pm till 10pm. She would meet me for my thirty minute break at 6pm when we'd go to a pub just around the corner. It

tea from a jam jar — Alfie Watson

was always great to see her but the time would pass so quickly that I often wondered if it was really worthwhile, after all, she would have had to rush home from work, get herself all glammed up and then head straight back into town, and all just to spend thirty minutes with me. I would always be late getting back to work and there was the odd night when I didn't bother to go back at all. I just couldn't bare to leave her, and whenever I did, I couldn't concentrate fully on the job. This absenteeism was soon picked up on by management and I was informed that my job would be in jeopardy if things did not change. After a few weeks we decided that we could not carry on like this for much longer and decided not to meet while I was on the late shift.

Twenty-eight

ON THE ROOF

Situated in the centre of Leicester, the views from the factory windows provided endless entertainment in times of boredom. There was always something going on outside to pass the time away. This was the era of the mini skirt and we were always guaranteed a great view of thighs and knickers of the passengers in the cars travelling about twenty feet below. The morning rush hour would see tens of lovely girls walking passed on the way to Corah, the largest hosiery manufacturer of the day. There was some real talent amongst them and every one would be greeted with endless wolf whistles as they passed the whole length of the factory. Looking back on this I realise it must have been really embarrassing for them, having to run this gauntlet of sexist hairy arsed men every day, the majority of whom would have been old enough to be their dads.

A new attraction was becoming the talk of the factory and was definitely getting everyone's attention. One knitter had discovered that if he were to go to the furthest point to the right of the knitting room, with the help of a telescope he could see into one of the student flats opposite, a distance of about 150 yards. Word soon got around the factory so as soon as the bosses had left, we were queuing up to see first hand if what we'd heard about what students got up to was true. And queue we did, often waiting in line for an hour or more. The telescope was extremely powerful and provided some really interesting views, in particular of a young girl aged around 20 years old who was totally void of any inhibitions and why wouldn't she be? Her rooms faced a brick wall across a narrow road of about 20 feet. So confident was she that she was safe from prying eyes, that she had no curtains at the windows. It wasn't long before someone discovered that if they climbed through the skylight in the toilets at the opposite end of the building, it brought them out onto a flat roof directly opposite the flats. The telescope was now defunct as far as I and the majority of us were concerned but it was still in use by some of the older blokes, who couldn't make it up to the roof. I was one of the first to the rooftop as soon as darkness fell. So there I would stand with my back against a brick wall, beer and fag in hand - the fag held in such a way that the glow would not be visible - with a perfect view into about three flats, all let to young nubile girl students. This was better than any porno film that I'd ever seen; this was utopia, with full sex and girls in various states of undress. One Chinese girl, who we christened the "Kinky Chinky", was really having a good time. She and her boyfriend appeared to be working their way through the Karma sutra and the way they were going at it, they would soon be on the final page. Parties were a regular event there every Friday night and throughout the weekend. There was often so much going on, it was impossible to know which window to look at. Almost the whole work force was on that roof, including the supervisor, all, without exception, with huge erections trying to burst from their trousers. Some of the married ones couldn't stand it and would feel the need to go home early. One in particular arrived home unexpectedly to find his wife in bed with another man.

During this period of moonlight porn, it became so easy to swap a late or night shift for an early one, and weekend overtime was always overbooked. Everybody wanted to work the late shift. It was great to see this free sex show every night but it was also very frustrating. I was now swapping my late and night shifts at every opportunity. I was constantly on early shift, and seeing Karen every day was better than any of the rooftop shows. One fact that had come to the management's attention was that production figures were falling dramatically during the late and night shifts and that perhaps breakdown payments were being falsified in an attempt to make up wages. Any breakdown claims had to be verified with the supervisor's signature before payment would be made. They were all as bent as nine bob notes and we had so much dirt on them that they could not refuse to sign. Boosted by the extra allowances for working unsociable hours, their earnings were reasonable but only slightly better than someone working the early shift, where allowances did not apply.

The bubble was soon to burst on the rooftop cabaret and all the bosses questions were about to be answered in one go. It had lasted for about a couple of months when some clumsy bastard fell through the skylight, smashing the glass and breaking a leg into the bargain. I don't know how he managed

tea from a jam jar   Alfie Watson

to talk his way out of that one, sooner him than me! The maintenance team, whilst repairing the skylight, saw just how much activity there had been on the roof by the evidence they took to the boss. There was cigarette ends empty pop and beer bottles and even a couple of chairs. This brought an abrupt end to the evening shows and also to the jobs of two supervisors. The skylight was now permanently secured and inaccessible. The only voyeurism available now was by way of the telescope which had somehow made it's way back into the knitting room by one of the few knitters not to manage the climb onto the rooftop, Sam was his name and the only reason he was not up there with the rest of us was because he had an artificial leg.

Things were never quite the same after this, with everyone's movements being monitored far more closely than ever before. And to make sure that this monitoring continued around the clock, they employed a team of dedicated security officers who missed nothing. Even my occasional trip to the pub during my tea break was now finally banned, on the grounds that drinking was not allowed whilst operating machinery. My pleas to management that I was not drinking alcohol fell on deaf ears. Nobody would be able to leave the premises at any time now without exception, during their shift, except in an emergency.

So, all the fun and games of the previous few months had come to an abrupt end, it seemed that the bosses had advised the students of what had been going on, even the flats had now got curtains, meaning the telescope was also rendered

tea from a jam jar *Alfie Watson*

useless. Whenever I bump into any workmates from that era, invariably the first topic to surface is the students, and they always remember to a man, the kinky Chinky.

Twenty-nine

BLACKPOOL

Once every year Karen's grandma would organise a trip to Blackpool and this year I was invited to join the coach along with all the old biddies from the estate. This was to be my first time there and I was really excited. I'd heard from the lads I worked with, what a great fun park it was and especially about how frightening the roller coaster was. The coach was to depart early Saturday morning for Blackpool and leave for home on Sunday afternoon. I was really so naïve in those days that all Blackpool meant to me was lights, and a scary roller coaster, that I was especially looking forward to riding. It was early September and coincided with the switching on of the lights, so the place was buzzing. This was a regular date every year and suited most of the group, who enjoyed a dance or two in the famous tower ballroom. The whole of the coach had been booked to stay at a hotel close to the Blackpool tower, couples obviously stayed in double rooms as did close friends. Karen would be staying with her gran and I was supposed to be with some old pensioner bloke I didn't even know. Karen, however had other ideas and within an hour of arriving she was dragging me around the shops looking for a cheap ring, that, I would later find out was to pass as a wedding ring when trying to get us a bed for the night. The council should have had other illuminations, in the form of giant road signs sited at the end of the M6 and other routes into Blackpool that weekend, stating that "WE ARE FULL UP"

I can't remember exactly how many hotels and guest houses we tried but it was quite a lot. I think we knocked on every door between the tower and the fun park. Eventually, after spreading our search to the streets behind the Golden mile, we got lucky after knocking on what seemed like a hundred doors. There were no vacancies at this latest address either, but we must have tugged on their heart strings because they asked us to wait while they made a few enquiries. Minutes later they came back to us saying that they had asked one of their friends to put us up and directed us to a property about two streets away. We had just spent the previous couple of hours pounding the streets of this Benidorm of the North West, whilst rehearsing our pretend names and our wedding date, just in case someone should ask. I know it sounds a bit predictable but I seem to remember it was to be, Mr and Mrs Smith. We really needn't have bothered because the couple who greeted us at the door were so kind and friendly and really only wanted to know our first names. We were welcomed with open arms and they treated us like their own. As this was to be the first time we had slept together, we were extremely keen to say our good nights and get to bed.

It was as I expected, a truly memorable night and one that the giant roller coaster could never match, and without doubt one that gave me an appetite for more of the same whenever I got the chance. We were awakened in the morning by a knock and a cup of tea and advised that breakfast would be ready in around an hour. After a hearty breakfast we said our goodbyes and left for the hotel where the rest of the party was staying.

As soon as we entered the hotel, we recognised a couple of people who we knew were on our coach and chatted to them, confirming the departure time. I was relieved now that at least if Karen's Gran did asked where we were last night, we could say that we stayed in the hotel and had witnesses who had seen us leaving early in the morning. I remember being genuinely concerned about this but Karen seemed not to care much about it at all and thought that I was being more than a little paranoid. She was absolutely right, I was paranoid and this was the fault of my upbringing and my parent's constant need to know of my every move. As it happened, her gran never asked, she was probably too pissed to notice. Anyway we headed off towards the fun fair to spend the last couple of hours before we had to get the coach back home. The roller coaster was certainly a big beast and it took all my courage to get on it but I'm glad I did, at least I'll be able to tell the blokes at work that I'd done it. This weekend had been brilliant and has given me a taste of life without my parents picking over everything I did and said, it was wonderful feeling of freedom.

Thirty

THE PROPOSAL

I can remember the day I formally proposed to Karen, it sort of just came up in conversation one night. We had gone to a new pub in the town centre called the Churchill and she was dressed in a beautiful black dress with lace sleeves and looked a million dollars. We were talking about one of her friends who had recently tied the knot, she asked would you? I replied, would I what? Would you marry me? My reply was, of course I would. And from that day we talked of little else for weeks. So really, she proposed to me in a way!

We both started working as much overtime as we could get and saving started immediately, with Karen in charge of the bank book. It was lovely to have a goal in life and I wanted nothing more than to spend the rest of my life with her. Everything seemed to be going along fine; I was still at home although still constantly under the threat of being slung out any day. I remember being surprised at how much we were saving and how quickly it was mounting up. This was driven purely because of the circumstances we found ourselves in, regarding our home lives. But it was Karen's amazing ability to save which made it possible. Something she has continued to this day. It was great fun buying things to put away for our future digs. This was referred to as, saving for the bottom drawer, I've never understood why. Any way these things were saved at my house because there was slightly more room than at Karen's house and perhaps a lot less risk of things being tampered with or broken. Life was good and I thought that my past would soon be put squarely behind me. I still met some of my old mates occasionally but these were getting fewer and further between, as they had mostly all now got girlfriends of their own.

When I was with Karen I was happier than I'd ever been and I knew that she unknowingly saved me from a life of crime, which, I had thought would be inevitable for a boy with my background. We often talked about being together and escaping from the lives we were living and decided that we would marry in the spring of 1965. Although we would not be able to afford everything we wanted immediately, we should be able to get quite a lot of stuff by buying second hand. I would have known her for about two years by this time. I know this is not considered by many people to be very long, but like all generations of teenagers, we knew what was best.

It wasn't long before a giant spanner was thrown right into our plans. Somehow my mother had discovered that Karen was a Catholic and she would not be considered acceptable for any son of hers, even one that it was obvious she didn't want or care too much for anyway. She had, overnight, overnight, become a devout Irish protestant complete with all the hatred that many of her kind bore for the Catholic Church. Amazingly she now pretended to care! My life now was like heaven and hell every day. Hell whenever I was at home and

tea from a jam jar *Alfie Watson*

heaven when with Karen. One day everything got out of hand and I found myself being thrown out yet again, only this time the "bottom drawer" (packed into various cardboard boxes) was also leaving, thrown via the front door into the garden. There was a lot of shouting and screaming from both my mam and dad as I struggled to collect them up, many of the ornaments and glassware items were broken. To make matters worse Karen arrived to witness me salvaging what I could. This was the first time she had seen first hand what they were capable of. With all our bits and pieces gathered up we headed towards her house. I knew they wouldn't want me there as they just didn't have the room. So rather than carry all this stuff to Karen's house I decided to see how the land lay at my grandma's. She was as welcoming as ever and after hearing of my plight, agreed to help me with bed and board until I found somewhere else, I was determined that I wouldn't get my grandma involved and I only stayed a few days until I found myself a self contained flat, vowing never to return home ever again. The flat owner lived directly below and did not encourage his tenants to have visitors, in particular the female variety. So it was basically just somewhere to lay my head. Situated about 3 miles nearer to the town centre it meant that at the end of a date and after walking Karen home, I would often arrive at the flat in the early hours of the morning, dropping exhausted and fully clothed onto the rock hard mattress.

This situation, while not ideal, had its benefits, the main one being that I no longer had to listen to my mother's rantings, and could come and go as I pleased. It also meant that I was going to have to cook for myself. There were no fast food outlets around in those days, no kebab shops, Pizza hut's or MacDonald's to resort to, apart, that is from the local chip shop which I must admit was a saviour now and again. The fact that we were both saving hard meant that living costs must be kept to a minimum, and if that included food then so be it. I would grab a meal from anywhere I could, my grandma would provide my Sunday lunch and occasionally Karen's mam would also invite me round on weekdays. I would survive somehow, after all if all our plans were realised we would be married in less than a year when our earnings would be shared.

Thirty-one

THE WEDDING

It was more important now that I keep my job, as there was the potential to earn a very good wage, if only I could get there on time. I had improved my time keeping somewhat in recent times, but due to my change in living circumstances, I was once again struggling and I knew it wouldn't be too long before I was on the carpet again. In order to eliminate the risk of being late I managed to find someone who would swap occasional days, usually around the middle of the week. However much I plotted and schemed there was no escaping the fact that my time keeping had to improve if I was to keep this relationship with Karen alive.

With the wedding day set for the 3rd of April 1965 I now had to knuckle down and make sure that I kept this job. It was now becoming quite rare for me to be late and I was also volunteering for as much overtime as I could possibly get. We had not booked the church yet because for some reason there had become a shortage of reception venues, so this took priority. This was the normal order that these things were done in those days. We eventually managed to locate a local pub, The Tudor, that had a room available, so we provisionally booked it and left a small deposit. Not the nicest of places but at least it was now ours for that date and it was a load off our minds. The ideal place to hold the wedding ceremony would be at the Blessed Sacrament Roman Catholic Church which had supported Karen and her family over the years.

With the passing of the weeks it became of paramount importance now to book the church as soon as was possible. We met with the Priest and provisionally booked the day. It would not be possible to have full Catholic wedding because I was a Protestant. It was explained that in order to receive the full blessing, which Karen would have really liked, It would have meant that I would have to change my faith and promise that any children born to us would also become Catholics. Whilst I could never consider myself to be a religious person, I was not prepared to make this pledge as I considered it to be a form of blackmail or possibly a recruitment drive. We both felt that our children would decide their own faith once they were old enough.

The next step was to arrange for a registrar to be present. Now the problems really began in earnest. Because of the fact that we would both be under the age of consent, which was 21, we desperately needed permission from our parents. Karen was aged 17 now and her parents signed without any fuss, whereas I would find it rather more difficult. I knew that I would not be welcome at home, so I wouldn't be able to just knock on the door and ask for their signatures, I was also aware that I might have to beg and plead once I did get to speak to them. I thought that once they knew that I would be staying a Protestant they would possibly sign. Purely by chance I bumped into my dad on the bus travelling into the town one day. I reluctantly approached him and explained the situation we were in and he agreed to fill in all necessary papers. He said we should call round the house the following day. I felt that he needed that time to work on my mother. Anyway, we arrived with the papers in hand but were unceremoniously escorted away from the door to the gate and were told by my mother who incidentally was pregnant again, that she would never give her blessing to such a union, and we should never show our faces there again. Karen was inconsolable, there was so much depending on them signing and time was passing so quickly, what would we have to do now?

This latest kickback really hit us both hard, not least because the venue for the reception was now requesting a second payment in order to secure the date for us. Obviously we would have to inform the registry office that we couldn't get the signatures and just see what transpired. They couldn't have been more helpful and seemed very understanding of the predicament we now found ourselves in. It was explained to us that we could be granted permission by the courts but it would need to have both of my parents in attendance. A date was duly set for around a week later in order to allow my parents to be notified by the court that their attendance at the hearing was requested.

That day came but unfortunately for us, my parents didn't. Can you imagine the stress we were now both under? Especially Karen, who, apart from all this aggravation, was also busy making two bridesmaid dresses for her sister and her niece and a pageboy outfit for her youngest brother, not to mention arranging the invitation cards. All this and working full time, I had to admire her drive. We were now well into February with the wedding only a matter of weeks away when we were advised by the registrar that they would now have to officially present a summons by hand to my parents, ordering them to attend another hearing, again about a week or so later. With just four weeks to go we were finally given "permission and best wishes for our future", by the court for the wedding to go ahead, and as you can imagine we were ecstatic.

My parents had defied the courts order to attend so the magistrate took the view that they obviously didn't care a jot about the outcome or they would have been there. We were so happy now; we felt that my family had done their utmost to ruin our plans and had failed. The papers were now shown to the priest and the bands were duly read each week for three consecutive weeks in accordance with the Catholic Church procedure. We decided that we'd ask my grandmother if she would stand in for my parents on this special day. She jumped at the chance and my uncles Alan, Gerry and Brian, aunties Pearl and Joan were also there, with Alan being my best man. Lots of friends, many from work also promised to attend. We would make this wedding special, no matter what!

We were married on April 3rd 1965 as planned, and the sun shone beautifully.

We had an amazing wedding day despite all the obstacles that had been put in our way. Karen looked fantastic, her wedding dress was beautiful as were the bridesmaids and the page boy in their tailor made outfits, she had worked so hard towards making this day special.

Unfortunately, as with most weddings, things don't always run smoothly. Usually it's one of the guests pewking up over someone unintentionally, or a lad who can't take his ale, wanting to fight the world. Someone demanding a drink after time. Food might run out, it could be that a glass of red wine gets spilt over the brides dress. It could be, but it was none of the above.

The one to put a dampener on this special day was the groom himself, who in his wisdom, invited three of his mates back to the flat for a game of cards, and then had the audacity to ask Karen to make them sandwiches!!! Not the greatest start to married life!

So it was clear that I still had a lot to learn about partnerships and sharing, if I was to keep this special girl.

I'd love to know what you thought of my first book.

alfie_watson@hotmail.net

16040030R00109

Printed in Great Britain
by Amazon